Supply Chain Management

Supply Chain Management Workbook

Francis Harrison

ELSEVIER
BUTTERWORTH
HEINEMANN

THE INSTITUTE OF
OPERATIONS
MANAGEMENT

AMSTERDAM • BOSTON • HEIDELBERG • LONDON • NEW YORK • OXFORD
PARIS • SAN DIEGO • SAN FRANCISCO • SINGAPORE • SYDNEY • TOKYO

Elsevier Butterworth Heinemann
Linacre House, Jordan Hill, Oxford OX2 8DP
200 Wheeler Road, Burlington, MA 01803

First published 2001
Transferred to digital printing 2003

Published in association with the Institute of Operations Management

British Library Cataloguing in Publication Data
Harrison, Francis
   Supply chain management workbook
   1. Business logistics 2. Production management
   I. Title   II. Institute of Operations Management
   658.5

Library of Congress Cataloguing in Publication Data
A catalogue record for this book is available from the Library of Congress

ISBN 0 7506 4999 2

For information on all Elsevier Butterworth-Heinemann
publications visit our website at www.bh.com

Typeset by Avocet Typeset, Chilton, Aylesbury, Bucks
Printed and bound in Great Britain

Contents

Introduction

Managing the supply chain is a competitive necessity in today's global marketplace where differentiation between products and services means providing a total value package that can compete for an increasingly discerning and empowered customer.

For those who do not grasp the importance of strategizing and managing the supply chain, the likelihood is they will increasingly feel the effects of market turbulence, where reactive alignment to the marketplace clock of opportunity, or catching up with the competition can have many costs.

Traditionally management of organizations, and more noticeably with large organizations, optimization of operations, of functions, was left to individual production and inventory units. Inventory has been used to buffer against incompatibilities of adjacent links in the logistics chain and against operational uncertantities. This traditional approach to buying, storing and making goods is a fragmented one.

Today's view is one of integration. Supply chain management is the integrated management of business links, of information flows and of people. Attention is given to the whole chain from raw material supply, manufacture, assembly and distribution to the end customer. The supply chain is viewed as a logistics channel, a thread which not only provides the means of getting goods, services and information to the customer, but also continually strives to do so in the most efficient and innovative way.

To achieve integration and innovation the managed supply chain must utilize the resources of technology and most importantly people. A fundamental development in supply chain management is the recognition of the need to create environments that fully involve all employees – and not just a minority involvement – thus encouraging integration and participation through management, awareness, and learning, shifting perspectives of participation from an inward functional viewpoint to the outward process viewpoint which looks to benchmark processes and actively identifies with improvement opportunities.

Management holds the key to the way the supply chain environment is shaped. Management can either 'pull' employees along, where employees have a 'limited' perspective of participation and rely on management to firefight problems that arise as there 'responsibility'. Management can also try to attract the 'best' employees. Again this type of strategy is likely to pull some employees along but not all, leaving too many employees 'rocking the boat' because they do not identify with change and the reasons for it.

Or management can become facilitators, creating the 'best' environment to get the 'best' out of all employees where management look to create a positive framework for participation by addressing the needs of the workforce, such as stability, enjoyment, responsibility, objectives, equality and identity within teams and the organization. In this environment the focus of management can be geared towards steering the company in the right direction.

Creating the best environment is an absolute necessity in an increasingly fast-paced marketplace. If the right environment is not created, and management continue to try to pull people along and spend too much time fighting fires instead of steering the company, then the fast-paced environment of the business world will lead to competitive weakness, disgruntled employees who have to react to increasing change without necessarily understanding the reasons, and a working environment which causes all a great deal of stress.

The objective of this book is to help with the integration process by raising awareness, perspectives and opportunities for innovative participation. The book has been divided into two parts. First, Chapters 1–14 provide an overview of the subject, discussing the components of a supply chain and the opportunities for improvement. Second, following on from the overview, a series of questions and pointers (checklists – Chapters 15–30) invite the reader to, either individually or in groups, become proactive in terms of self-appraisal and company performance assessment.

Abbreviations

BOM	bill of materials
CRP	capacity requirements planning
DRP	distribution resource planning
EDI	electronic data interchange
ERP	enterprise resource planning
ISO	International Standards Organization
JIT	just in time
KPI	key performance indicator
MPS	master production schedule
MRP	materials requirement planning
OEM	original end manufacture
OPT	optimized production technology
PC	personal computer
RCCP	rough-cut capacity planning
WIP	work in progress

Chapter 1

The end customer

The end or final customer is the person at the end of the supply chain who makes the decision whether or not to buy the product or service offered. The purchasing decisions of the end customer have some proportional effect on each facet of the supply chain contribution to the finished product.

It is the end customer that brings profit to the supply chain. Profits for the supply chain are dependent on the customer's purchasing decisions and on the efficiency of the supply chain to produce the product. Each process, either internally or externally, should be adding value to the product. Processes that do not add value diminish the levels of profit that can be achieved. The levels of profits that can be achieved and the continuation of these relationships form the basis for managing and integrating the supply chain.

Perceptions generally about who the end customer is may vary along the supply chain. Take a manufacturer for example, employing hundreds of people. From the supply-base perspective the manufacturer for day-to-day transactions may well be regarded as the end customer. Given that this perspective prevails, the manufacturer is perceived as the 'responsible' entity for communicating demand – where satisfaction begins and ends.

The perception that satisfying the demands of the next customer is the end of the supply obligation is important. In the above example the manufacturer might supply an original end manufacture (OEM). The OEM in turn might integrate the supplied product into its own product for supply to a distributor. The distributor then adds value to the product by marketing it to attract the end customer. One begins to understand that any one link, whatever its scale, must 'accept' responsibility for improving the information flows and understanding of the needs of the other.

The inward perception fails to realize the importance of the customer–supplier relationships throughout the total supply chain. Moving attitudes away from ownership detachment to an outward view that realizes the importance of the end customer in all aspects of the supply chain will help to make the supply chain more efficient and responsive to the needs of the customer.

Understanding the customer

To understand the customer there must, first, be some direct link with the customer and, second, it is essential that these information channels 'speak the language' of the customer. Learning what frustrates or delights the customer can be done on a one-to-one basis or in groups, with surveys and interviews. Information about customers' preferences, buying habits, attitudes toward particular products and service satisfactions can be collated to form 'scientific' customer profiles, which are not based on assumptions and perceptions.

Getting closer to the customer, compiling information about the customer's first enquiry, repeat ordering patterns, service satisfaction and customer attitudes will provide the inputs for designing the product and value package that matters to the customer. Knowing what matters to the customer will help align the supply chain towards meeting and exceeding customer expectations.

In markets where demand exceeds supply (seller's market), it may be 'acceptable' to align business attitudes along the lines of 'make a product then sell it'. In a seller's market, competing for the end customer may focus the organization's resources on internal excellence, i.e. the product, reliability, quality, price and relative lead time.

In today's marketplace, global competition has increased capacity to produce products. The result is excesses in supply and equality of physical products. This increased capacity, coupled with a more discerning customer, means that producers must focus on excellent internal and external performance.

Figure 1.1 lists some differentiating attributes. The left-hand column contains the product (internal) related issues. The other three columns list a variety of issues that are not product related – these are external performance related. The internal and external benefits which can be provided are part of the competitive need to develop the supply chain in order to realize the maximum benefits that will form the total value package.

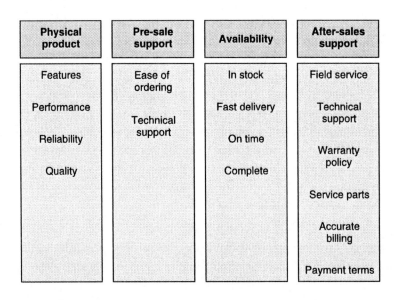

Physical product	Pre-sale support	Availability	After-sales support
Features	Ease of ordering	In stock	Field service
Performance	Technical support	Fast delivery	Technical support
Reliability		On time	Warranty policy
Quality		Complete	Service parts
			Accurate billing
			Payment terms

Figure 1.1 Differentiation attributes
Source: Mather (1998).

Retaining the customer

It takes five times as much effort, time and money to attract a new customer than it does to keep an existing customer (Christopher, 1994). One study of the car market in the USA found that a satisfied customer stays with the same supplier for a further twelve years after the first satisfactory purchase and during that period buys four more cars. To the car manufacturer this level of customer retention is estimated to be worth $400 million per annum in new car sales.

Research (Christopher, 1994) has shown that retained customers are more profitable than new customers, for the following reasons:

1 The cost of acquiring new customers can be substantial. A higher retention rate implies that fewer customers need be acquired and these can be acquired more cheaply.
2 Established customers tend to buy more.
3 Regular customers place frequent, consistent orders and therefore usually cost less to serve.
4 Satisfied customers often refer new customers to the supplier at virtually no cost.
5 Satisfied customers are often willing to pay premium prices for a supplier they know and trust.

6   Retaining customers makes market entry or share gain difficult for
    competitors.

The customer's purchasing decision will take into account the total
value package on offer, i.e. the total or differentiating attributes compared with a competitor's similar product. As part of the decision to
make the purchase the customer will have some basic expectations.
For example, the product must be 'fit for purpose'. Adding to the
value package something so new or a feature that was not anticipated
by the customer will exceed the customer's expectations and he or she
will be delighted with the purchase.

   Satisfying the end demands of the supply chain whatever the
product or service offered is not only a moving target, but increasingly
today's basic needs were yesterday's unexpected delights. It is an
important fact that the features that delight the customer today will
gradually move towards spoken needs, and eventually become basic
expectations:

1   *Basic spoken needs*: these are the needs the customer regards as so
    elemental they do not need mentioning. If these needs are not met
    the customer will be dissatisfied.
2   *Spoken needs*: these needs might be requested features that the cus-
    tomer would like as part of the total value package. They are
    options that will satisfy the customer.
3   *Unspoken needs*: these are unexpected delights. The customer had
    not anticipated this attribute as part of the value package.

Retention of customers is the focus for 'relationship' marketing
(Christopher, 1991). Customer retention has many benefits, including
development and alignment of the total value package. The principle
of relationship marketing is that the total package offered to the customer comprises a core product and a service package that surrounds
it. The idea is to create such a level of customer satisfaction that the
customer is unlikely to look for an alternative supplier. The shift to
relationship marketing is shown in Figure 1.2.

The internal customer

The internal customer is an internal delivery partner, processing parts
for the next operation. Treating internal customers as delivery partners is a recognition that we must understand their needs and expec-

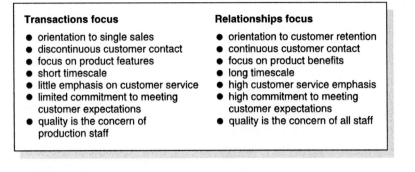

Transactions focus	Relationships focus
• orientation to single sales	• orientation to customer retention
• discontinuous customer contact	• continuous customer contact
• focus on product features	• focus on product benefits
• short timescale	• long timescale
• little emphasis on customer service	• high customer service emphasis
• limited commitment to meeting customer expectations	• high commitment to meeting customer expectations
• quality is the concern of production staff	• quality is the concern of all staff

Figure 1.2 The shift to relationship marketing
Source: Christopher (1991).

tations. The partnership approach shifts the focus for daily activities from an inward perspective to an outward perspective, raising individual and collective responsibility for eliminating wasteful practices at every opportunity, and in doing so delivering the right parts at the right time to the right place to the right quality to the next operation.

The delivery partnership is a culture of listening and improving. Employees are encouraged to raise ideas and suggestions, and take responsibility for their work and their development. The company should provide education and training programmes that help employees identify with the goals and objectives of the company. Employee integration requires communication and recognition. This is emphasized by the company setting common measurements which make progress and improvements visible for all to see. Objectives are shared and achievable, and work activities are planned and measured.

The supply partners

The external supply base is an integral part of the supply chain game plan. Often, however, suppliers are treated as a distinct entity and kept at arm's length, the driver for communication being supply disruptions and reactive cost reductions to marketplace conditions.

Typically a medium to large-sized company spends in excess of 50 per cent of sales revenue on purchased items. The integral clarity of procurements ability to source from the best suppliers, and the best suppliers' ability to meet the demands of the customer has been obscured by the traditional confrontational approach, encompassing:

- distrust of suppliers
- competitive tendering
- a lack of knowledge about what components or services should cost
- a lack of real ability to focus on management of suppliers
- narrowly focused objectives
- lack of awareness of causes of waste
- short-term business horizons
- 'macho' business mind-set.

The Japanese have led the way in realizing the importance of customer–supplier relationships. They have developed collaborative arrangements for all aspects of mutual involvement. This has enhanced the range of services that the supplier is able to offer. The supplier becomes an integral part of the supply chain strategy, taking responsibility for product design and development, warehousing and inventory management, cost-reduction initiatives and customer–supplier cross-functional skills sharing.

The form of partnership may vary. For example, it may comprise some degree of financial integration through minority equity or outright purchase, or preference will form the basis of a partnership. Whatever form of partnership is deemed appropriate, fundamentally it should be based on long-lasting and mutually beneficial understanding, together achieving business growth and success at the expense of the competition. In this respect they will work together to eliminate waste in all aspects of their transactions. They will work together in cost transparency mode. Each partner knowing about the other will produce understanding of the elements of product cost, quality and any consequential problems that may arise.

`Chapter 2`

Manufacturing in essence

Essentially manufacturing and, indeed, the supply chain are a flow of information and materials, illustrated in Figure 2.1. In essence the objective of manufacturing is to improve and speed up the flow of information and smooth the flow of materials.

Information flow	Planning, control, execution, through closed loop systems, linking with suppliers, the rest of the company and the customer
Material flow	Suppliers to customers, a pathway of business links and processes adding value

Figure 2.1 Flows of information and material

The speed of information flow can literally be at the speed of light. For example, computers, fax machines and telephones can connect information exchange 'immediately'. Where information flow is a people-managed activity the rate of flow is slowed. The rate and management of information flow becomes dependent on people intervention and individual responsibility, and may depend on a number of variables affecting its management, such as workloads, attitudes, and so on. Effective information flow is a prerequisite to effective material flow, and both need to be accurate, swift and balanced.

Effective information flow must be freely directional, travelling to where it is required and received back to wherever it is required. Messages and feedback need visible pathways so that any information flow breakages can be identified.

Material flow and flexibility are a synonymous necessity for the competitive supply chain. Fast-paced change is a way of life for business. Flexibility is the management of reacting to changes in demand by preserving the resources of time, money, materials, people, plants and suppliers until they are specifically required.

If flexibility is to be achieved, it will require faster and smoother flows of information and materials. Therefore, the control of manufacturing should be a balanced strategic macro-managed entity, i.e. the whole of manufacturing is managed without functional imbalance. All the needs of manufacturing must be satisfied, not just a few.

Where the flow of information and material is an integrated managed activity, the greater the clarity needed about which steps should next be taken to improve flows still further. For example, operating a just in time (JIT) system necessitates a high degree of information and material visibility. A manufacturing environment which is a chaotic, disjointed, functionally introverted enterprise will undoubtedly lack the necessary focus on the benefits of visible and speedy flows of information and materials.

Chapter 3

Changing market forums: the Internet

The Internet is an integration of multimedia sources – the merger of words, graphics and application tools providing a forum that is a television, newspaper, computer, shopping precinct, workplace, school, and so on. It is a composition, a matrix of connected computers around the world advancing global communication opportunities and immediacy of information flow. Previously mute computers can now talk to each other.

Web-enabled personal computers (PCs) will transform information technology into a primary medium for human communication as hundreds of millions of PCs are or will become connected. The Internet provides a company with the facility, regardless of its own scale, to advertise, display and demonstrate its products. It also gives customers multiple choices about their purchase decisions, and provides ready information about competitors, new products and technologies.

For the business community this is a medium that is making available product offerings to a wordwide market at any time of the day, 365 days a year. Not only do the business processes become accelerated as customers' perceptions about availability become a real-time delivery expectation as a spoken need, but the total value package will also have to make provision for customer interactivity with the supply chain, providing access to information about stock availability, pricing, progress tracking and delivery date confirmation at the time of order, which will need to be competitive wherever in the world the order is received.

The global enterprise used to be the domain of a few companies whose scale could give them production, procurement and branding benefits that could compete with 'local' competitors overall, if not on lead times. Those advantages are fast disappearing as lead time becomes ever more important. A major issue for all supply chains will be their ability to compete within local markets. The customer expectation will be determined by local benchmarks, which means satisfying customers irrespective of their location. This raises a key issue, that of logistics. How do we get our product or service to the customer in the most competitive way? This is discussed in the logistics overview in Chapter 13.

Another perspective of the changing nature of supply chains as a result of the Internet is the extension of supply chains through the connection of consumers to the process. The customer is able to interact with the supplier, from ordering to tracking delivery. This interaction and further integration possibilities are changing the supply chain model. Some companies have been able to alter the supply chain or value chain model by removing a series of business links (Figure 3.1).

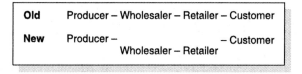

Figure 3.1 An altered supply chain or value chain model

Some computer companies for example have developed after-sales support and customer service practices by automatically upgrading the customer's software with the latest releases. Registration of the purchased product brings the customer closer to the provider and increases the opportunity for selling additional services. It also provides the customer with greater support, such as contact numbers for assistance and even 'automatic' fault diagnosis. Overall this could alter the supply chain or value chain model with a series of links removed to form a developer–customer model.

The Internet is not only a medium for interaction with the marketplace. It also provides the opportunity for business relationships to be enhanced. Intranets and extranets are other examples, summarized in Figure 3.2.

The Intranet is a company-based information-sharing facility. Take a sales force as an example. Their distinct locations can be connected to the company through the Internet via laptop computers. This connectivity can help improve the efficiency of the sales force by bringing

	Intranet	Extranet	Internet
Environment	Restricted-access Company-based sharing	Semi-restricted Secure Available to supply chain partners	Unrestricted Public domain

Figure 3.2 Mediums for interaction with the marketplace

them closer to the customer. Customer service can be improved with real-time communication from the customer to the organization about order processing, product configuration, availability, tracking, and so on – real-time order processing.

Extranets are another supply chain communication enabler, helping supply chain partners to communicate, and exchange data together. They can become 'linked' entities readily sharing real-time information and enhancing service provision such as customer service, technical support, order and inventory management, and product and service tracking and delivery.

Intranets and extranets can help change the supply chain model as a series of linked self-interests where 'distance' can affect relationships and communication. Continuous electronic communication can enhance clarity and value creation to the supply chain where information exchange becomes a real-time activity, helping to raise awareness about waste, bottlenecks and misunderstandings. These facilities are available now and will help deliver real-time value innovation throughout the supply chain.

Chapter 4

The product

The focus for the traditional competitive comparative advantage was the physical product, i.e. functionality, reliability, quality, price and lead time. The focus of supply chain management operating in today's global buyers' market is on providing a total value package that is inclusive of the physical product. However, this does not detract from the importance of the physical product. In today's buyers' market the physical product is a core element of the evolving total value package.

Business necessity must stimulate demand decisions. Understanding customer needs and facilitating moving expectations, together with differentiating the total value package strategies, require a greater frequency of 'reinvention' in relative time today than it did yesterday. Therefore, management of the supply chain must incorporate into its business planning, shorter product life cycles, quickest time to market for new products and continually meet or exceed customers' expectations.

The product and manufacturing sector

The importance of the product in terms of competitive differentiation of the total value package will depend on the commodity marketplace and the performance drivers. That means that a differentiating feature that is deemed important to the customer will depend on the application of the product. This incorporates the application, marketplace differentiation and the designed for manufacturing perspective.

Their are four major manufacturing sectors, illustrated by the Puttick grid (named after its originator, John Puttick) in Figure 4.1.

1   *Commodities* comprises simple nuts and bolts. The product design is probably simple. Volumes are high and the goods are widely

available. For this type of product, market price will be a competitive differentiator.

2 *Durables* are likely to be complex products and may consist of a wide variety of variation and features. For example, audio equipment, televisions and cars, offering diverse features such as colour, engines, sunroofs, and so on. Differentiation in this sector will be the best value for money total value package. High product variety and cost competitiveness will most likely require a flexible manufacturing base that can offer product variety through latest possible product definition or by modular methods. Product design for manufacture and flexibility are key business strategies in this sector.

3 *Jobbing and fashion items* will include short-lived appeal products such as one-off novelty items. Competitive advantage is likely to be determined by the product concept, design and timing. In this arena, product design through to product availability will need to be achieved in the minimum time to maximize the window of opportunity.

4 *Capital equipment*: product performance is a key business winner in this sector. The product, e.g. an aeroplane, must expressly meet customers' needs and it is of paramount importance that a close partnership between supplier and customer is achieved. The topics for inclusion in the partnership will certainly include product development and incorporation of leading technologies.

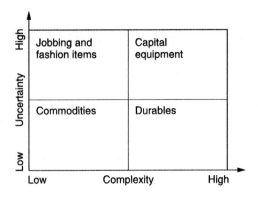

Figure 4.1 The four major manufacturing sectors
Source: Croner (1999).

Product development

Product development is a synergy between the customer, marketing, sales, product design, production, purchasing and vendors. The desired result of this synergy is the development of a product that will at least meet the customer's expectations, which is significantly dependent on marketplace windows of opportunity, and can be produced to deliver profit.

A traditional product development programme is one where functions interact sequentially with the product development process. Marketing information is passed to the product designers. When they have added their value the project is passed on to the process designers, then to production, then to purchasing, and so on. Whatever the exact flow, the point here is that the design process is a fragmented sequential functional flow.

The drawbacks of the traditional sequential product development programme include the likelihood of detachment of the customer perspective with its input from the marketing information from which the product was likely originally commissioned. As the product is developed, assessed and 'improved', passing from one function to another, the final product developed may not be what the customer actually desires. A product that is developed which is not what the customer wants will increase the pressures on the sales function to sell, making forecasting even more difficult.

It is not only the customer that becomes detached as a result of the product development sequential flow; communication between functions is hampered. As one function receives the product, criticism about former functions' contributions are likely, after all, the next function is charged with carrying on where the previous function left off. The objectives of any one function may not be understood by some other function.

Sequential product development is opposed to the main component of the programme – delivering what the customer wants in the best possible time. Varying perceptions and stifled communication flows will, as a consequence, require extra degrees of rework on the product either prior to launch or post-launch. All this has the effect of either elongating product launch or affecting customer service and market reputation. The market opportunity that was initially present may have moved on, which will then necessitate further reactive development.

Supply chain management is largely about integration, communication flows and elimination of waste. It follows, then, that product development must also be an integrated communicative and value-adding activity. The needs and wants of the customer must be known, shared and developed by integrated teams formed across functions on a product-by-product basis.

Link	Explanation
Customer <–> Marketing	Customer needs and wants. Customization. Forecasts.
Marketing <–> Sales	Definition of product objectives. Customization. Sales objectives.
Marketing <–> Product design	Definition of product objectives. Customization. Refinement of product design.
Product design <–> Process design	Manufacturing of the product. Product design. Customization.
Product design <–> Manufacturing	Manufacturability of the product. Make/buy decisions. Product design.
Process design <–> Manufacturing	Manufacturability of the product. Production routing. Production methods.
Product design <–> Procurement	Manufacturability of the purchased components. Make/buy decisions. Refinement of product design.
Marketing <–> Manufacturing	Refinement of product objectives. Forecasts. Customization.
Procurement <–> Vendors	Manufacturability of the purchased components. Production forecasts and schedules. Quality requirements.
Manufacturing <–> Vendors	Purchased components. Shipment scheduling.
Manufacturing <–> Sales	Production scheduling. Orders. Order status.
Manufacturing <–> Procurement	Production scheduling. Quality requirements. Shipping requirements.
Sales <–> Customers	Orders. Production information. Order information.

Source: Tomkins (1989).

Table 4.1 Winning manufacturing product development explained

The product teams are a representation of needed contributory functions and may include: marketing, sales, product designers, process designers, purchasing, manufacturing and vendor representation. Figure 4.2 emphasizes the possible advantages of a successful product development approach. The team will be able to assess the degree to which product change is required, from a tweak to a complete new product, and will 'live' with the task from preliminary design through to its successful production. Table 4.1 offers brief summation examples of the interactional agendas of the team.

Winning manufacturing product development	Traditional product development
Faster to market	Slower to market
More manhours in product development	Fewer manhours in product development
More expensive product development	Less expensive product development
Less manufacturing cost	More manufacturing cost
Superior product performance	Inferior product performance
Superior product acceptance by marketplace	Inferior product acceptance by marketplace
Preferred approach	Obsolete approach

Figure 4.2 Winning manufacturing and traditional product development compared
Source: Tomkins (1989).

Because all the functions are working together simultaneously and know the wants and needs of the customer, the product development process is likely to be quicker and better received by the marketplace, promulgating the company's presence. By reacting quicker than the competition to the needs and wants of the customer, control of the marketplace is more decisive thus forcing the competition on the defensive.

Quickest time to market, product performance and customer acceptance are clear advantages. In this context some disadvantages need to be understood and accepted. For example, the product development teams require the dedicated resources and interactions of a wide variety of functional participants. The consequence may be that this approach will cost more than the traditional sequential approach. Figure 4.3 highlights the degree of interactivity of the cross-functional manufacturing product development approach.

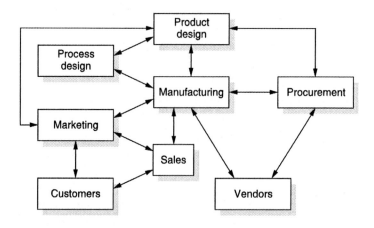

Figure 4.3 The interactivity of the cross-functional manufacturing product development approach   *Source*: Tompkins (1989).

However, whether acceleration of the product development process will add cost is a perception or a reality, gains may offset losses. One example is that acceleration of efforts is an increase in participation and focus where previously the utilization of resources was not so effectively channelled.

Product development measures

For some companies there may be a tendency to be reactively driven, i.e. they react to customers' complaints, react to shareholders, react to competitors and react to new business initiatives on the basis that others are ahead by using a particular technology or system therefore 'it must be the right thing for us to do'. For this particular discussion we are talking about product development, but the logic applies to all facets of business management and strategy – define and make clear objectives, and measure the benefits. Data-driven activities provide a better framework for continuous development than do 'quick fix' judgements.

Measuring the product development activity quantitatively can help balance objectives. Product development requires a host of resources, and where resources are required trade-offs ensue. Quantifying the objectives of the development of a product programme will help to focus on and balance such issues. There are four key product development objectives (Figure 4.4).

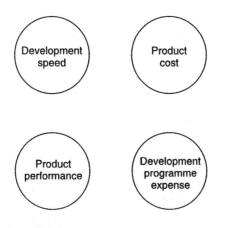

Figure 4.4 The four key objectives
Source: Smith and Reinertsen (1991).

Product introduction and time

Speed or time to market should be a measure from when someone first starts work on the project up to the time the project becomes a product available to the customer. Inclusive in the development cycle time should be the time that the product proposals have been submitted, design approved and prototypes developed. Including these parameters in the product development cycle will enhance the quickest time to market focus, so that each time a conceptual product idea is presented the product development clock starts ticking.

Figures 4.5, 4.6, 4.7, 4.8 and 4.9 are examples of the trade-offs that are likely to exist between speed and cost. By creating a model of the

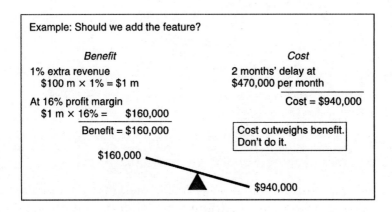

Figure 4.5 Trade-offs between speed and cost: example 1
Source: Smith and Reinertsen (1991).

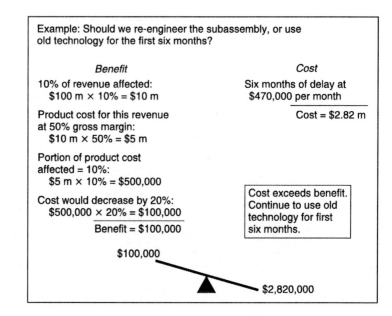

Figure 4.6 Trade-offs between speed and cost: example 2
Source: Smith and Reinertsen (1991).

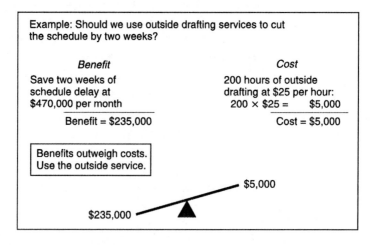

Figure 4.7 Trade-offs between speed and cost: example 3
Source: Smith and Reinertsen (1991).

product development process the trade-offs can be agreed and targeted as part of an overall performance strategy.

Getting products more quickly to the market can benefit the alignment between the product attributes and shifts in taste or the effects of economic and political influences. The marketplace from a product development perspective is a balance between time (the market clock)

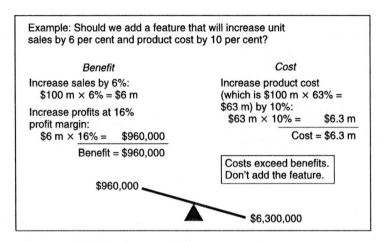

Figure 4.8 Trade-offs between speed and cost: example 4
Source: Smith and Reinertsen (1991).

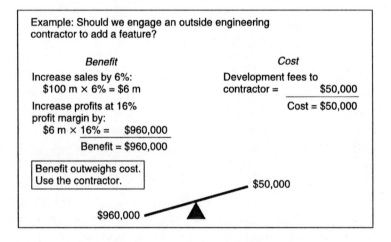

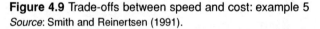

Figure 4.9 Trade-offs between speed and cost: example 5
Source: Smith and Reinertsen (1991).

and opportunity (an open window). When the need for a product becomes apparent in the marketplace, or where technology advancements can be utilized for product 'invention' their is no turning back – when a latent need in the marketplace has been stirred, the marketplace clock ticks away while that 'need' is satisfied.

The objective of product development is the synchronization between the project's clock with the marketplace clock. If the project is started late, or has overrun, the project clock might effectively run behind the marketplace clock, which may effect product positioning and sales opportunities.

A company that has been first to introduce a product into the marketplace installs a sense of urgency into the competitor perspective, but for the competition the apex of opportunity in the marketplace may already be passing. Getting to the market first provides an invaluable education for the market leader to build on, as it is able to obtain further advantage by refining the product to satisfy the customer, and thereby align itself with the market potential. Coming second in the marketplace makes product alignment much more difficult.

Another advantage in introducing products quicker to the marketplace is the extension of sales information. For each month that development cycles are reduced the same period could be added to the product's life, extending revenue and profit. Manufacturing also gains by being ahead in the manufacturing learning curve so that early advantages of the product introduction continue through the stages of its life cycle and, possibly, on to the next product introduction.

Time is increasingly becoming a measure of opportunity for improvement and benchmarking. In automotive development the Japanese have achieved considerable cycle-times advantage over a substantial portion of the competition in the west. Continuous cycle-time advantage helps create entry barriers for the competition because of the strengthened position of market entrepreneurship. Continuous cycle-time advantage also creates increases in the generations of advantage. For example, suppose a Japanese manufacturer is able to develop a car in forty months compared with competitors who take sixty months. For the Japanese manufacturer this is a ratio advantage of 3:2. Extrapolating this as a continuous advantage means the Japanese manufacturer would have a nine-generation advantage compared with competitors' six generations, with all the associated benefits of branding, learning curves, pricing freedoms, and so on.

The Japanese speed of product delivery to the marketplace has, in part, been a result of the strategy of a faster but small-step approach to product definition. The marketplace is treated as a learning curve experiment. Introducing the product to the marketplace provides opportunities for learning what needs to be changed in order to satisfy the customer, which helps align future generations of products more accurately. This learning by doing approach is managed by the ability to make numerous but small design changes, gearing product development to actual market response.

Focusing on product development as one mega-project carries with it enormous learning curves for everyone involved, and makes development cycle times long and unpredictable. The mega-project has to fit on to the base project a host of new elements, each of which have to interact with a number of existing elements, so as the project grows adding new elements becomes increasingly difficult. Product development strategy may depend on the type of product involved but, whether one mega-project or a small-step approach, emphasis needs to given to quickest time development and market delivery.

Global product development

A world product is not a product that without some local customization can be sold around the world. McDonald's, for example, serves a different hamburger in Germany than it does in England. IBM has over twenty different keyboards for satisfying markets by country. Product development for the global marketplace must comprise a standardized product platform combined with flexible manufacturing and logistics systems. Global product development must consider the needs of distribution to the customer from a single or small number of bases in the world, or as core product distributed around the world for final configuration. Global product development is a key business strategy for the globally competitive supply chain.

Chapter 5

Mass customization

Mass customization uses the platform of supply chain management to focus on the individual demand requirements of the customer. Mass customization is a customer-integrated supply chain that does whatever is necessary to develop, produce, market and deliver low-cost customized services and products, as illustrated in Figure 5.1. By managing the value chain better and faster more opportunities are created for learning, so that the better, faster supply chain moves closer each time to giving the customer precisely what they want, or at least sustaining the divide between customer expectations and delivery.

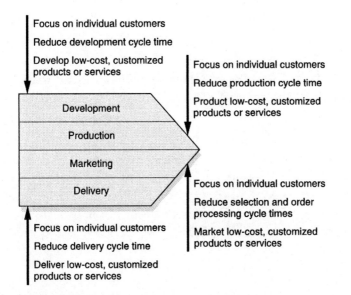

Figure 5.1 Culmination of changes in an organization to mass-customize products and services   *Source*: Pine (1993).

Mass production and mass customization

The mass production environment is typified by a focus on efficiency through stability and control. Mass production has developed into providing goods that nearly everyone can afford by increasing the efficiencies of developing, producing, marketing and delivery. However, the rate of technological change, increasing customer expectations, shorter product life cycles, the global marketplace and an information explosive environment not only means that competition is tougher but the marketplace has, and is, becoming increasingly more turbulent and fragmented because, as more and more customers demand tailored solutions to their demands, they in effect become a portfolio of niche markets, which is not an environment suited to the mass production system where customers are placed at the end of the value chain.

In the mass-customized system the customer is placed at the beginning and the end of the value chain. The ideals of mass customization share the goals of developing, producing, marketing and delivering goods and services with the mass production system but, in addition, tries to offer enough variety and customization so that nearly everyone finds exactly what they want.

Satisfying the customer's individual needs and wants inevitably means proliferation of the product variety offered. For the value chain, proliferating variety in order to satisfy most if not all customer desires fragments the marketplace. Greater variety must be achieved with greater flexibility.

To compete in the dynamic mass-customized environment, the processes of development, production, marketing and delivery take on as great, or greater, importance than the product itself. This is because with so much product variety potential the individual product may decrease in importance. The effect is a decoupling of the product and the process life cycle. The process life cycle outlasts the product life cycle. It is the process life cycle that is important because the process can be used again to produce new products.

Mass customization strategy

For some companies the road to mass customization is an evolutionary process of incremental improvements. Depending on the competition, this approach may be quite satisfactory. However, competition that leads the way in mass customizing its products will cause great turbulence for any competition found wanting. The turbulence will manifest itself in lost sales, fluctuating demand and increased customer expectation.

For some organizations the market turbulence may be so great that the only way to stay in business is for the company to transform itself, either making significant changes in a relatively short time or creating a totally new business that can offer a customized service from start-up, combining technology and strategy. For others the move towards mass customization may already exist within the organization. Indeed, even unknowingly. Functional dynamic leadership may 'pull' other areas of the business into making gains as an organization, but this is no substitute for an overall managed strategy.

Customizing the standard product

Within the value chain of a product, four basic elements exist: development, production, marketing and delivery. Taking a standard product and customizing it is possible by altering one or more of the elements in the value chain. For example, an aeroplane seat is a standard product, but by altering the marketing and delivery elements of the product, offering business class and first class, with options such as personal movies, laptop computers and so on, and including other services as extras but at an additional cost the experience becomes a mass-customized experience, a tailored solution. Even booking the tickets can become a mass-customized experience from booking by phone, fax, e-mail, via the Internet, from the home or office.

A razor introduced by Gillette which 'automatically' adjusts to the contours of your face is an example of a standard product, but designed to satisfy the individual customer. The author recently bought an off-the-peg suit. The trouser legs, though, were too long. As part of the standard service the retailer offered to adjust the length of the legs to suit my requirements. This is an example of point of sale customization. Within an hour the trousers were ready, so I could carry on shopping without inconvenience. Had it been necessary to wait a day or two the point of delivery concept would have lost its appeal, unless I was given a choice. For example, photographs can be developed in an hour at a price premium or in two to three days for the standard service and price.

Information is an important medium that can be used to customize the standard product. The 'information industry' can help collate information about the customer, and takes the volume of standard information available and customizes it. The customer encounter becomes a learning experience. Information collection and analysis can be used to develop and customize the product or service to better fulfil the needs of the customer.

Modular mass customization

An analogy of modular mass customization is a standard letter comprising a core or base module – a standard format. We can add modularity by incorporating dates, recipients' names, addresses, alternative paragraphs, and so on. A module should be an addition to the core product. For example, mix and match paints whereby a base colour can be used to which are added other colours to form a specific colour requirement for the customer – customizing the final colour from modular blueprints. Modules can be replaced with other modules. Redesigning a module is easier and quicker than redesigning the entire product. As products proliferate, particularly as the number of variations approaches the number of individual customers, the greater is the cost advantage of modularity.

Chapter 6

What is forecasting?

Forecasting is the 'science' of predicting demand. The forecast is generally formulated either from historical trends where past performance is 'scientifically' extrapolated into a future predicted trend, or from market information that considers potential sales in a particular market, perhaps as a result of some market-changing event. For example, will road fund licence reductions for vehicles with engines up to 1100 cc affect the levels of demand for smaller cars?

Forecasting is the formulation of a statistical matrix that may be derived from sales data analysis, which would include the determination of details such as product ratios, seasonal variations and product life cycle position, then extrapolated for trend analysis and strategic planning. The raw statistical data requires interpretation by sales and/or marketing to assess variable factors such as new product launches by key competitors, planned price increases and any details that may have influenced base data about sales. Without this review the forecast based on historical data alone could be highly unreliable

A forecast, however competently collated, is still a prediction. Its accuracy will need to be tracked against actual trends. The forecast is a best estimate of likely sales used to assist decision-making processes in areas such as strategic planning, budgeting, resource allocation and investment.

Indirect extrapolation

Forecasting future demand for a product with no previous history could be achieved by assessing the number of potential customers. For example, suppose the new product in question is a cough mixture. Historical sales and trends of similar products could be assessed. Any such data could be used to assess the gender, age, seasonal variations, and so on. Spare parts demand is another example where data could be calculated. A fan-belt demand for example could be assessed from knowing how many cars fitted with this particular fan-belt have been sold, together with information about expected sales for the end product (the car), and should also consider data about the service life of a similar or typical fan-belt.

Direct extrapolation

This form of 'prediction' takes into account past sales data. Past data can be modelled and extrapolated to gauge future trends. The three most commonly used forecasting techniques are moving averages, weighted averages and weighted averages with trend.

The moving-averages method uses historical data from previous periods over which demand has remained stable. The average performance of the selected periods is then used to predict the future demand.

The weighted averages method uses both old data and the latest available (current sales) information. A forecast used for the previous period can be used for the next period by updating the previous period in light of the current period's demand.

The weighted averages with trend method seeks to improve the weighted average technique by introducing more variables into the forecast formula, thereby capturing among other things trends in underlying demand.

Effects of aggregation on forecast accuracy

Forecasting a group of items is more accurate than a forecast for individual items. For example, determining a forecast for a whole work centre throughput can compensate overall for the loss of activity in one area by the extra activity in another area.

The same applies to the advantages of forecasting over the long term rather than a detailed forecast. This means that a forecast over a year is likely to be more accurate than a forecast for a particular month throughout the year. This is best illustrated (see Table 6.1) by calculating the standard deviation (assuming sales are independent), i.e. the deviation between the forecast and actual sales over a range of past periods.

The formula is

$$\sigma = \frac{\sqrt{\Sigma i \, (Fi - Di)^2}}{n}$$

where σ is the standard deviation, Fi and Di are the forecast and demand for period i, and n is the number of periods considered.

Month	Forecast	Actual sales	Deviation	(deviation)^2
1	115	117	−2	4
2	105	110	−5	25
3	105	115	−10	100
4	115	120	−5	25
5	115	110	5	25
6	105	90	15	225
7	125	115	10	100
8	125	133	−8	64
9	125	126	−1	1
10	135	130	5	25
11	135	130	5	25
12	135	144	−9	81

Table 6.1 Examples of deviation between the forecast and actual sales

The deviation column is the difference between forecast and demand. Each value is then squared (which makes the + or − sign irrelevant). The sum of the squares is then divided by the number of months. This gives the average square. The square root of this figure gives the 'root mean square' or σ.

Table 6.2 is a comparison of deviation between forecasted and actual sales over a one-month period and sales over twelve months.

Month 6	12 months
Average = 105 units	Average = 700 units
Standard deviation = 15 units	Standard deviation = 58.33 units
Sales deviation ranges = 75 and 135 units	Sales deviation range = 1424 and 1456 units
Deviation = +/− 28.6%	Deviation = +/− 1.12%

Table 6.2 Comparison of deviation between forecasted and actual sales

Calculating standard deviations and forecasting manually is not really necessary. Many information technology forecasting packages are available which are capable of modelling complex data for forecasting and tracking accuracy on an ongoing basis. The formula has been included here to emphasize the 'science' between aggregation and the correlation of forecasts.

The accuracy of forecasts is something that needs to be continually or consistently measured and variables about the forecast investigated. Efforts need to be made in order to understand causes of inaccuracy so variables become predicted variables that provide realistically predictable tolerances about what can be expected from the forecast and are shared with all parties that depend on the accuracy of this information. Wherever possible, though, solutions should be sought for reducing dependency on forecasts at the operational level.

Forecasting using information technology

Forecasting requires the dissemination of complex data. Historical sales will comprise some aspect of economic persuasions, effects of promotions, of seasonality, of product ratio variances and product life cycle position. Forecasting using information technology provides a mathematical dissemination of sales data, which can be modelled to show trends (Figures 6.1 and 6.2). Extrapolation of these trends can be used to predict future sales.

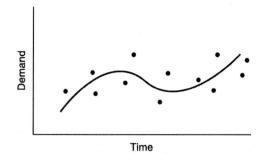

Figure 6.1 Mathematical dissemination of sales data, modelled to show a trend: example 1

Product life cycle modelling and positioning can also improve forecast reliability where current trend analysis could be misleading (Figure 6.3).

The forecasting package should integrate with the other areas of the organization. Capturing data for analysis, modelling and

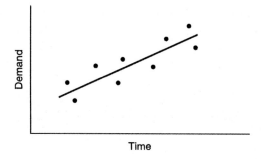

Figure 6.2 Mathematical dissemination of sales data, modelled to show a trend: example 2

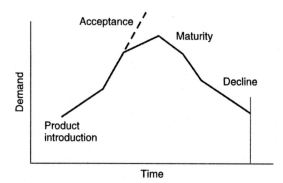

Figure 6.3 Example of product life cycle modelling and positioning

strategic planning requires information about sales, marketing, production, capacity, inventory, purchasing, lead times and distribution planning. The forecast package should have the ability to automatically update forecasts, provide business reporting, what-if simulations, forecast accuracy tracking, identify major shifts in demand, product life cycle positioning, and should be easy to use and understand – a transparency about how forecasts are derived and what they mean.

Forecasting with the customer–supplier

Part of the forecast input will have been derived from direct contact with the customer. This information provides a valuable insight into the customer psyche in terms of their plans, preferences and needs. Customer profiles can predict the future and explain the present.

Passing forecast information to supply partners is vital. 'Squandering' information and information delays will add cost and uncertainty along the supply chain. This is most prevalent where the ethos of supplier partnering and the relationships of supply chains have not yet been realized.

Forecasting and the supply chain

Initiatives to make supply chains more responsive to demand have focused attentions on flexibility, speed and dependability. Some of these advantages have been achieved by supplier partnering, quality assurance, pull systems for material flow and scheduling, including electronic data interchange (EDI) communication, and reductions in lead times, set-up times and lot sizes.

However, forecasting is still an important focus, especially where the customer lead time is less than the supply lead time. The data (Figure 6.4), from research carried out in 1995 by the Economist Intelligence Unit, emphasizes that forecasting is a key focus for businesses re-engineering their business processes and remains so for many companies at the start of the twenty-first century.

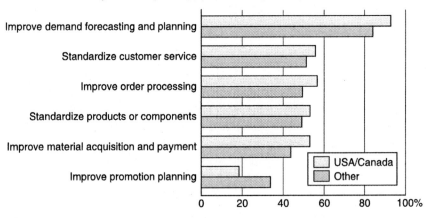

Figure 6.4 Forecasting for business process re-engineering
Source: Kruse et al. (1995).

Revising forecasts regularly will help reflect the latest knowledge about future demand. Removal of political pressures from the forecast is also important for understanding demand. For example, frontline sales personnel might produce forecasts which are low and, therefore, readily achievable as a sales target. Sales managers might produce too high forecasts to spur on subordinates. Alleviating political persuasions is a task for top management. Getting the forecast environment right is very important. In this respect responsibility for forecast assimilation should be assigned to either a forecast manager or the master production scheduler so that any hidden agendas can be removed from the forecast. However, it is unlikely that forecasts errors can be eliminated altogether, therefore attention must be given to improving systems for responding to forecast inaccuracies.

Chapter 7

Customer order management

A customer placing an order sees the business primarily through the order management process. It is therefore essential that the order management system is able to facilitate timely and complete order fulfilment. The elements of an integrated order management system are broadly outlined as:

- defining customers, options, end items, pricing and taxes
- status tracking
- picking
- packing and shipping
- invoicing and accounting
- after-sales technical support.

The order management system in today's time-sensitive marketplace should consider the implications of shortened product life cycles and reductions in lead times, with JIT assembly and deliveries. For example, order quantities – does the system have the flexibility to cope with the range of customers demands placed on it? Delivery frequency – is the system able to respond quickly within closely specified time-windows and frequent deliveries?

Carl Sewell in his book *Customers for Life* (cited in Christopher, 1994) says: 'Being nice to people is just 20 per cent of providing good customer service. The important part is designing systems that allow you to do the job right the first time.' Consistent product and service delivery creates the possibility for a continued relationship.

Order management is an interface with the customer. Therefore, it is important that efficiency and fail-safes are part of the integrity of the order management system. An example of a fail-safe is being asked by a utilities company to have with you certain information ready before calling, e.g. your reference number, post code and so on. This is a measure of efficiency and fail-safing the integrity of the interface. If the customer supplies the wrong information, where fail-safes are not in place, the perception from the customer's view is likely to be one of poor service because the interface has somehow broken down. The Japanese call fail-safing *poka yokes* (from *jokeru*, 'to avoid', and *poks*, 'inadvertent errors'). By addressing fail-safes it is possible to identify critical points in the order entry, planning and delivery process. If something goes wrong, for example, a stock out, the whole delivery on time process will be affected.

Order cycle time management

The order cycle time is the time that elapses between receipt of the customer's order through to delivery. One aspect of order cycle reduction fulfilment is to eliminate manual steps and replace these with an integrated automated system which provides speedy information and linked procedures, improved information flows and order commitments. The complexity of an order-promising and delivery-commitment fulfilment is suggested in Figure 7.1, which is a simplification of the routines that a customer order will travel to reach a satisfactory conclusion.

An automated order cycle broadly integrates the following areas:

1 *Customer service*: integration with planning and scheduling systems. Order entry provides available-to-promise information on line with immediate item allocation, including price confirmation for standard and custom orders; item options configuration from a database selection; on-line status reports; remote customer order entry capability for enhanced customer communication.

2 *Materials management*: integration of order entry requirements into the materials functions for accurate available-to-promise scheduling; system distinguishes firm orders from forecast orders; customer order throughput status tracking and shortage reporting into customer service function for customer notification.

3 *Finance and accounting*: customer order information flows immediately and automatically to accounts receivable.

4 *Distribution*: provided with information about due date commitments; carrier scheduling; provides pick lists by location, by order, by customer and produces 'picked complete' information.

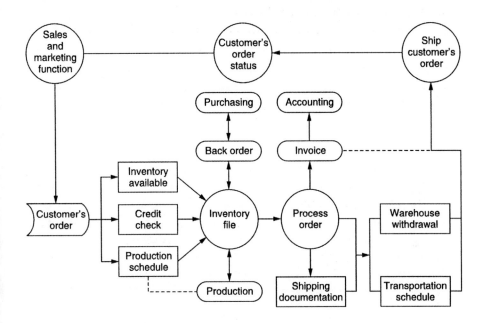

Figure 7.1 The path of a customer's order
Source: Christopher (1994).

Order entry automation and integration into the production and delivery functions of the organization can reduce order cycle times, improve the accuracy and integrity of the planning and scheduling processes, and improve order promise commitments.

Integration with production and delivery systems

One could argue that good customer service means either 100 per cent or 0 per cent, meaning that customer orders are fulfilled complete and on time, or they are not. However, organizations typically will have a standard of customer service measured as a percentage of 100. Whatever the exact percentage figure, it should be measured and opportunities sought for improvement. The service-level figure is a demand-management recognition of resource and feasibility constraints, and is a benchmark of the efficiency and effectiveness of the production and delivery management function's ability to fulfil demand complete, on time and competitively.

It must be understood that anything less than a 100 per cent customer service level implies that occasionally there will be an occurrence of a stock-out. This fact needs to be understood. A statement of service-level objectives requires management to recognize that a service-level desire of 100 per cent, together with a 'keep the inventory low' instruction with an intolerance when a stock-out occurs, is simply going to focus a great deal of attention on a given customer order transaction to remedy a particular problem. An emotional, knee-jerk response is not the solution – management is.

Order promising and service-level maintenance provide the basis for honest communication with customers. Customer loyalty is better served when the customer is told when to expect delivery – and is able to rely on it. To achieve this it is vital that demand is managed so that the integrity of order promising is sustained. Demand management is the activity managing the day-to-day interactions between the customer and the company. Demand management must merge all externally and internally generated demands on capacity, and integrate processes and information flows that will make possible timely and 'honest' customer-order promising.

Chapter 8

What is demand management?

Demand management is the link between manufacturing and the marketplace. It is a communication channel through which customers express their demands, and manufacturing 'guarantees' what it can commit to. Demand management encompasses forecasting, order delivery date promising, order entry and physical distribution.

Demand management must take into account factors that may affect demand, and therefore resources, such as economics – political and fiscal, pricing strategies, product alignment, promotional opportunities and business objectives. Sources of demand such as service parts, intracompany requirements and pipeline stocking must also be taken into account. Understanding market requirements and the sources of demand is vital if manufacturing is to allocate resources effectively and efficiently.

Demand management is the spotlight on the integrity of manufacturing's ability to fulfil its commitments to the customer. It also demonstrates manufacturing's competence to plan and control all quantities and timings of demand placed on it. More precisely, it is a pointer towards the degree of management focus and hierarchical co-operation about the objective need for a planning cultural environment, where demand, both firm and forecast, only consumes available capacity. The better demand can be managed and the better resources can be planned and allocated, the better the 'honest' order promises that can be given to the sources of demand.

Managing demand involves accepting, or not, orders which may degrade honest order promising given to other customers. A customer base will comprise customers who have greater influence than others, most likely because of their particular volume of business. However, informal bargaining about priorities should not prevail. Instead, customer promising should follow a set of rules for approval, to protect the integrity of the demand management function. An approval system should ideally include higher-level management review, agreeing or not schedule changes, and communicating and enforcing procedures for order entry and delivery date promising, while considering the effects the mix changes may have on all production and delivery integrity – a set of rules which everyone plays by which can prioritize a customer, but also consistently gives 'honest' order promises within realistic service levels.

Demand and customer service levels

The demand management perspective of good customer service should include delivery on time and the speed or lead time of availability. There are three types of lead time:

1 *Customer lead time* is the time taken between customer ordering and customer receipt.

2 *Production lead time* is the time from the ordering of all materials for end items production, until the last operation is complete.

3 *Manufacturing lead time* is the time from material availability at the first manufacturing operation until the last manufacturing operation has been completed.

A company that consistently misses its orders commitment cannot rectify the problem simply by extending its customer lead-time promises. For example, analysis of the product throughput in manufacturing shows that orders are consistently one week late. A ready solution might be to extend the customer lead time by one week. However, it might be reasonable to assume that because the lead times have been extended the customer base will react by increasing or bringing forward their orders to compensate. Backlogs ensue and the strategy has failed.

Lead times, it must be said, are to a degree what management makes them. They can be managed and improved, but at the discretion of management – measured in terms of staying in business 'acceptability'. With management will, a company can transform itself either from a point of lengthy lead times or by further building on core strengths as part of a supply chain management strategy.

Management will is one aspect of a competitive and dependable response to demand. However, a planned demand management system must include a strategy for the 'best' order promise to the customer which utilizes resources effectively and cost-efficiently. Trade-offs with this strategy include speed, dependability and cost. Increasing speed, for example, must not put undue pressure on dependability otherwise the objectives of speed are lost.

Demand management must balance the optimization of resources, including capacity and inventory management, against the 'benefits' of holding large inventories with capacity availability excesses that would enable order fulfilment of any unanticipated demand to be added within lead times into the order book. The cost of having available capacity and inventory which could cater for any unanticipated demand is unlikely to be competitively viable. Therefore, management should either accept the demands of the customer and live with chaos, or manage demand by understanding what levels of customer service can be achieved within existing constraints.

Sources of demand

Knowing the sources of demand is important if the right material and capacity resources are to be planned effectively. Sources of demand might include intercompany demands such as warehousing replenishment, comprising distribution allocation considerations, spare parts requirements, new product items, other product item life cycle considerations, promotions and so on. For demand management to allocate the right resources to fulfil firm and anticipated orders, any individual forecasts and information about demand must be brought together so that the collation of demand is consistent and the whole equals the sum of the parts.

One method of addressing this issue of a co-ordinated and integrated forecast about demand where demand is derived from a number of sources within the organization is to consider the pyramid forecast approach (Figure 8.1). Level 3 begins with individual forecast items, and is rolled up to forecasts for product groups into level 2. The product groupings are then rolled up into level 1, from which the total business forecast is an aggregated sum of levels 3 and 2. Level 1 forecasts are considered and finalized by top management for formalization of the business plan. This plan can then be forced down (constrained) into the product groupings and individual items which produces a forecast (as previously discussed, forecasting aggregates or product families is more accurate than forecasting individual items)

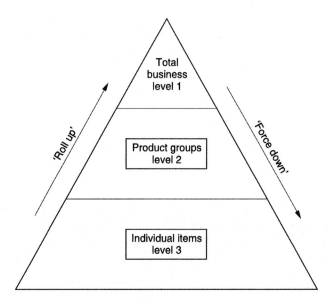

Figure 8.1 The pyramid forecast approach
Source: Adapted from Newberry and Bhame (1981).

that is consistent with the level 1 plan and considers all sources of demand.

Integrating marketing and manufacturing

The marketing function is primarily manufacturing's link with the 'attitude' of the marketplace. It is therefore essential that marketing communicates effectively with manufacturing the customer's desires about the product and the total value package, and includes product values, response times, order sizes, order frequency, packaging requirements, and so on. Only through discussion between marketing and manufacturing is it possible to achieve realistic customer expectations against what it is economically viable to achieve, and communicate this back to the customer.

Information about what the customer desires, if communicated regularly to manufacturing, will help determine what should be produced, how to produce it, how to package it, what mode of transport should be used and when to ship it – aligning manufacturing to customer desires through market interaction. If integration with marketing will help manufacturing understand customer desires, then manufacturing must help marketing understand the parameters of customization that can be handled economically. The traditional relationships between marketing and manufacturing must change if the stereotypical view of each function prevails, as suggested in Figure 8.2.

Marketing should understand the effects that end of month, end of quarter and end of year flurries have on manufacturing's order fulfilment integrity. Integration of functions should include marketing responsibility for co-ordinating promotions with manufacturing so that these programmes can be realistically and economically handled. Integration should include a co-ordinated approach to new product introductions, their start up and forecast alignment.

Forecasts are an important feature in manufacturing's efforts effectively to plan resources, particularly in an environment where the customer lead time is less than the supply lead time. Manufacturing should clearly understand what levels of accuracy they should expect from a forecast. Marketing and manufacturing must work together not only on short-term production scheduling, but also on long-term capacity forecasts.

What manufacturing believes about marketing	What marketing believes about marketing
Marketing desires low-cost, high-quality, instantaneous delivery and unlimited options even though the marketing forecasts are inaccurate. In general, marketing people are uninformed and don't actually understand the reality of business.	Marketing is in touch with the ever-changing, unpredictable desires of the marketplace and has a true understanding of how to make the company successful. Marketing has positioned the company very well in the marketplace in spite of the lack of support from manufacturing.
What manufacturing believes about manufacturing	**What marketing believes about manufacturing**
Manufacturing has done a tremendous job of working with too little capital in creating a manufacturing machine that, given the proper notification, can respond to any reasonable production schedule. Manufacturing produces products at a quality level, consistent with their design and at a minimal cost.	Manufacturing would like to run the same product, without any changes, forever, and still would not be able to produce at a quality or cost level that would satisfy the customer. In general, manufacturing people are lazy, unimaginative, and really don't care about the changing needs of the marketplace.

Figure 8.2 A stereotype view of the manufacturing marketing war
Source: Tompkins (1989).

Demand management responsibility

Responsibility for the organization of demand management might be an activity performed by more than one function within the organization. For example, the finance department may have to determine credit worth of a customer demand by performing credit checks. The customer services department may be responsible for order entry and order bookings. Outbound distribution of customer orders could be the responsibility of the logistics function.

For some firms the materials management function has the responsibility for the flow of materials from raw material supply through to production processing and shipment on to the customer. In this environment demand management could be an integral part of the materials management function. In a marketing-orientated firm demand management may be performed by the marketing or sales functions. In a product-development orientated environment close contact between engineers and customers might be better served by management of demand by the technical services department.

Whatever function or functional integrated perspective is deemed appropriate, the emphasis must be on responsibility of ownership and the transparency this affords the objective of fulfilling orders complete and on time.

Chapter 9

The master production scedule

The master production schedule (MPS) is an anticipated build schedule for end products or product options which extends into the future for at least as long as the cumulative lead time of the products contained in the build plan. It is a statement of production rather than a statement of demand, i.e. although it may include forecasts for determining the MPS, the MPS actually differs from the forecast. The MPS takes into account planning requirements capacity limitations and the desire to utilize capacity effectively. To achieve this, items may have to be built before they are needed for sale.

The MPS is the 'best' disaggregated top-level production plan that drives the dependent demands on the materials requirement planning (MRP) system. It provides a matrix of what production should make in order to satisfy demand responsively, but also does so in a way that will optimize the utilization of resources. The MPS matrix must understand what capacity is available to produce the goods against how much demand is required, and when.

The MPS is the company's game plan, a strategized game plan, which forms the basis for determining manufacturing, and sales budgets. The formulation of the MPS considers bottlenecks within the production flow – potential capacity issues – demand requirements and timings. With this information decisions about order promising and trade-offs between what manufacturing can do and what marketing would like to do can be agreed.

The MPS record

Table 9.1 is an example of a time-phased MPS record. The forecast in this example is projected at 15 per week, 20 are on hand at week 1. The

MPS is scheduled at 15 per week to achieve an available or closing stock of 20 units each week. How much stock is deemed appropriate will depend on details such as forecast accuracy, production levelling between inputs and outputs, actual production throughput against plan, and so on.

Week no.	1	2	3	4	5	6	7	8	9	10	11	12
Forecast	15	15	15	15	15	15	15	15	15	15	15	15
Available	20	20	20	20	20	20	20	20	20	20	20	20
MPS	15	15	15	15	15	15	15	15	15	15	15	15
On hand	20											

Table 9.1 An example of a time-phased MPS record: a levelling strategy

Table 9.2 illustrates an MPS for a seasonal demand. The MPS is adjusted to the marketplace demand.

Week no.	1	2	3	4	5	6	7	8	9	10	11	12
Forecast	10	10	10	10	10	10	20	20	20	20	20	20
Available	20	20	20	20	20	20	20	20	20	20	20	20
MPS	10	10	10	10	10	10	20	20	20	20	20	20
On hand	20											

Table 9.2 A chase sales MPS approach to seasonal sales

Table 9.1 is a 'levelling' strategy. This type of strategy should not call for capacity adjustments or changes in resource requirements because variances in forecasts have been catered for. Table 9.2 is a 'chase' strategy. This type of MPS will require adjustments to production to chase the demands of the marketplace, in this case, seasonal changes.

Table 9.3 is an example of a chase MPS with lot sizing. A batch of 30 is triggered when the available balance gets to 10. In this example the lead time between releasing an order and completion is one week. The goal is to find the MPS plan that best balances costs and effectiveness to satisfy demand.

Week no.	1	2	3	4	5	6	7	8	9	10	11	12
Forecast	10	10	10	10	10	10	5	5	5	5	10	10
Available	30	10	30	20	10	30	25	20	15	10	30	20
MPS			30			30					30	
On hand	20											

Table 9.3 Lot sizing in the MPS

Managing the MPS

The MPS should be in equilibrium between the sum of the MPS and the whole of the production plan. The MPS should not be a wish list – an overstated MPS. Overstating inputs against actual output ability will undoubtedly degrade customer order promising. Production throughput will then become a priority list decided by the lateness of an order, customer complaint or the need to juggle with critical ratio formulae's-time remaining (for due date completion) divided by work remaining. In the haze of decisions/chaos, transparency about the objectives of the MPS will be compromised.

The MPS can be thought of as the pulse of the company. If the pulse is running too slow, resources are not utilized effectively and potential orders could be turned away unnecessarily. If the pulse is running too fast, a backlog of orders is likely together with excessive work in process and priority lists. To achieve a stable rhythm to the pulse, understanding and agreement between the forces of market demands and manufacturing means of supply must be achieved. This fiat of understanding requires the highest echelons of management participation and support about how best to achieve a balance between inputs and outputs which is the best-fit overall.

MPS revision

Forecast inaccuracy is inevitable, so frequent review of the MPS is vital if the MPS is to reflect actual conditions. Table 9.4 shows a situation from week 1 through to week 12, using the MPS from Table 9.3 as the original data. No material was received in the first week because it was not asked for. However, demand has been revised for week 2, from the forecasted 10 units to 20 units, so actual closing stock at the end of week 2 will be 0 units instead of 10 as planned.

In Table 9.3, a 10-unit trigger inventory logic was used to establish a material requirement on the master schedule. To satisfy demand in Table 9.4 a lot size of 30 will be required in week 2 instead of the original MPS requirement in week 3. Questions will need to be asked about the feasibility of pulling the order forward. The lead time for a batch of 30 is only one week, but can this change in demand be factored into available capacity in that week?

Week no.	1	2	3	4	5	6	7	8	9	10	11	12
Forecast	10	20	10	10	10	10	10	5	5	5	5	10
Available	30	0	20	10	30	20	10	35	30	25	20	10
MPS			30		30			30				
On hand	20											

Table 9.4 Revised MPS after one week

The higher than expected sales in Table 9.4 should raise questions about the accuracy of the current forecast further out. Table 9.5 shows a revised forecast by marketing, and agreed with manufacturing, having decided that the original forecast in Table 9.4 is no longer relevant.

Week no.	1	2	3	4	5	6	7	8	9	10	11	12
Forecast	10	20	20	10	10	10	10	10	5	5	5	5
Available	30	30	10	30	20	10	30	20	15	10	35	30
MPS		30		30			30				30	
On hand	20											

Table 9.5 Revised MPS to accommodate forecast revision after one week

What can normally be added to the MPS is largely determined by time-fences. A time-fence specifies in periods or buckets what types of changes can be handled. The MPS might comprise two or three time-fence parameters. The furthest out time-fence might allow for any or reasonable changes to an MPS, where its likely that demand is mostly forecast rather than firm. The shortest time-fence might be quite rigid allowing only some minor change to a model series provided component parts are available, or it might be a frozen time period where no changes are allowed. Somewhere in the middle of the two extreme time-fences might be another which allows for one end item to be substituted for another, provided component parts are available and the production plan is not violated. Stability in short-range manufacturing plans is essential, especially where the customer lead time is less than the supply lead time. However, too few changes can lead to poor customer service and increased inventory. The objective is to strike a balance where stability is managed but with measured flexibility.

Capacity planning

The objective of capacity planning is to know what loads can be placed on a work centre at a point in time and in what order – a balance between load and capacity, although they do not have to balance exactly, but load should not exceed capacity. Scheduling work centre requirements to make a product requires a routing file. This specifies the operations and associated resources for a specific product from the ingredients in the bill of materials (BOM).

Planning available capacity at 100 per cent of current demand, though, is unlikely because demand will shift and some flexibility will be needed to satisfy changing market conditions, particularly in a JIT environment where some capacity is sacrificed in favour of the pull system of work flow.

Planning order acceptance or load timings requires information about the product's structure (routings and cumulative lead times). Figure 9.1 is an example of a product structure. It takes just one week to make part A. However, part A comprises parts B, C, D, E and F. The C and D levels have a lead time of two weeks, which go into the making of part B which itself has a lead time of three weeks. Parts B, E and F then form part of the product A. In all, the cumulative lead time to make product A is six weeks.

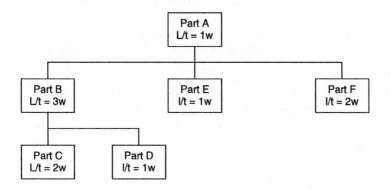

Figure 9.1 An example of a product structure

Accepting the limits of capacity is an important recognition that order management and the MPS are managed activities. The aim is to utilize resources effectively and to fulfil orders on time and complete. Deficient measurement of capacity will degrade those aims. Capacity planning or management is a balancing act between order acceptance and resource optimization. In the long term, capacity planning should address what levels of resources will be required. In the medium term, capacity planning should set the production programme requirements. In the short term, it is a detailed load and sequencing action plan. Whether long, medium or short term, the capacity plan should optimize the balance between the equation of load and capacity.

Capacity requirements planning

Capacity requirements planning (CRP) is a detailed load profile on capacity availability, which factors into the planning scenario all known variables. It is a time-consuming process, assessing 'all' constraints between timings, load sequencing and capacity. If capacity is not sufficient CRP should provide the data needed to focus on increasing or levelling capacity. This will help assess whether work patterns need adjustment, whether set-up times could be improved, whether there could be better maintenance planning, better job sequencing, and so on.

Rough-cut capacity planning

Rough-cut capacity planning (RCCP) is a quick way of assessing whether the MPS is achievable. It provides a way for the master scheduler to assess the feasibility of any proposed changes to the plan. An RCCP can quickly assess the feasibility of any MPS changes by comparing load scenarios with particular capacity bottlenecks or, in overall terms, by using known actual capacity availability.

Bill of materials

The bill of materials (BOM) are a set of ingredients which identify specific material requirements, either bought in or assembled in house. However, to construct a finished product the ingredients require a recipe – routing file – which identifies what materials are required, and in what order. Figure 9.2 is an example of the BOM recipe. To produce the top-level 0 or finished product, in this case a calculator, the material requirements are exploded through to the lowest level, 3, which comprises raw material and purchased parts.

Level	Item	Quantity	Type
0	Calculator	1	Assembly
1	Processor	1	Sub-assembly
2	Casing	1	Sub-assembly
3	Keypad	1	Purchased
3	Fasteners	6	Purchased
3	PCB assembly	1	Purchased
3	Inserts	4	Raw material

Figure 9.2 A bill of materials example

In this simplistic example of a BOM, a series of levels show what material is required and where in the process it is required. Level 3 items, comprising raw material and purchased parts, are assembled into level 2 items. Level 2 items are assembled into level 1 items. Then level 1 items are assembled into the level 0 item to form the finished product.

The complexity of the BOM will largely depend on the product and or type of manufacturing environment. In a complex environment the BOM would be fundamental to the MRP II system, indeed the BOM is fundamental to any MRP system. The point about degrees of complexity can be illustrated by comparing the balanced demand BOM and the structured demand BOM. The balanced demand BOM (Figure 9.3) shows a situation where very few sub-assemblies are required to form the final product. The components are assembled in a short space of time, except that is for sub-assembly which may have been assembled some time in advance of assembly. The balanced demand BOM is a JIT BOM – as the throughput speed of the manufacturing

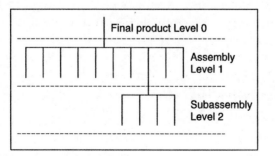

Figure 9.3 Balanced demand
Source: Croner (1999).

processes increases, the BOM becomes flatter, i.e. the process is more assembly than manufacture.

The structured BOM however, might comprise a number of sub-assemblies prior to assembly into the final product. Figure 9.4 is an example of a structured demand BOM. The process of producing the sub-assemblies through to completion of the final product may take several days or weeks. The variety of sub-assemblies increases the need for planning and logistics movement and storage.

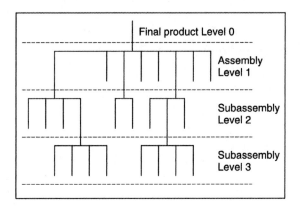

Figure 9.4 Structured demand
Source: Croner (1999).

Planning bill of materials

The planning BOM (Figure 9.5) can be applied where forecasting the completed item is impractical because of the numbers of optional variations the customer could choose from. In these circumstances it is more practical and manageable to forecast by product family. A car for example will comprise a body, doors, engine, catalytic converter, and so on. Past usage history and market research can provide information about the best ratio mixes by product family. For example 40 per cent of engines will be 1400 cc and 60 per cent 1600 cc. This is expressed in the planning BOM (Figure 9.5) 1400 cc engines, quantity 0.4 and 1600 cc, quantity 0.6. This same logic can be applied to the number of doors required, etc.

A planning BOM, or 'super bill' as it is known, when the top-level product is a composite of all the possible variations, provides primary information about specific material and assembly requirements and is an important concept in the management of the MPS.

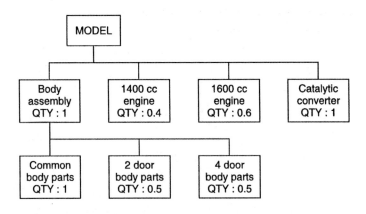

Figure 9.5 Planning bill of materials

The manufacturing environment

Construction of the MPS may vary, depending on the business environment. The manufacturing environment can be divided into three groups: make to stock, make to order and assemble to order. The primary difference between the make to stock, make to order and assemble to order firms is the definition of the MPS unit. However, many firms operate in more than one manufacturing environment. This is likely because a single environment is often inappropriate for the whole range of their products.

Make to stock

The make to stock environment produces what is required in batches, carrying finished goods inventory for most, if not all, end items. The MPS is a schedule of which end items should be produced and when. The end items can be grouped into a model type. For example, a consolidated item number can schedule items which are identical except for the finish colour. In this way configuration of end items is more closely aligned to a demand requirement.

The MPS in the make to stock environment is relatively straightforward, basically matching demand to available capacity. Making a finished or defined product for stock though can only really be justified where the customer requires such a fast turnaround that the goods have to be available before an order is received. Ideally, with the aid of planning BOM, the MPS schedule becomes a straightforward conversion into a final assembly schedule which is simply the substitution of one end item for another.

Make to order

In general the make to order company carries no finished goods inventory. It is likely that a large number of possible production configurations could fulfil a customer order, and therefore accurately predicting or anticipating a particular customer order requirement is unlikely. In this environment customers expect to have to wait for order fulfilment which will comprise a manufacturing lead time and, possibly, a design lead time. Stating an MPS requirement may therefore be difficult since design of the order may take place as construction takes place. Essentially the customer order is likely to be loaded on to the MPS in the first available capacity slot.

Assemble to order

The assemble to order firm is typified by an almost limitless number of end item configurations, all made from a basic design or sub-assemblies. Customer delivery time requirements are often shorter than total manufacturing lead times, so production must be started in anticipation of a customer order. Having a large number of end item configuration possibilities makes forecasting exact end item requirements very difficult, and stocking end items very risky, since they may have to be reconfigured.

Manufacturing flexibility is a key asset here. Therefore, it is advantageous to be able to state the MPS in terms of the planning BOM, such as an average requirement for a particular model series. In this way the MPS has as its components a set of common parts and options. Manufacturing flexibility means being able to configure the product as late as possible in order to satisfy a specific customer demand. Methods may include close integration of the order entry and order promising systems, partial anticipated assembly, and generic product design, including modular configuration and modular BOM – component sharing optimization into the product design.

MPS measures

The author has had experience with companies who measure MPS output in terms of monetary value. The problems observed from this experience are that some customers, whose products were more diffi-cult or time-consuming to make, suffered poorer delivery. Also meas-uring output as a monetary value and achieving that target was a greater focus than demand management and order processing.

Measurement of the MPS must be done in a uniform, concrete way that reflects the fundamental goals of the company (which must include customer service performance). The exact measure of MPS performance may vary between industries and particular companies. It may be an evaluation of how long a customer has to wait for a spe-cific end item. This will indicate how well the production plan has been disaggregated. Or it may be in terms of output performance against budget as a unit measure or a measure of customer service in distribution in terms of the percentage availability to deliver a cus-tomer order from inventory. Whatever measure is used performance indices should demonstrate the fulfilment of customer service level objectives.

Enterprise resource planning (ERP)

Integration of businesses, scale and differentiation will increasingly focus the organizational direction on marketplace branding, creating a 'total experience' for the customer from one diversified or world-wide organization. Creating one image for the total range of products from a range of manufacturing sites means fulfilling orders within balanced lead times with 'complete' on-time delivery. No single man-ufacturing site should adversely affect the total experience, hence the reason for mentioning enterprise resource planning (ERP) here.

Enterprise resource planning can be thought of as an umbrella strategy for integrating semi-autonomous business units within the organization. It is the enterprise-wide integration of MRP II sites pro-viding the opportunity for corporate management to co-ordinate planning across multiple sites by integrating the functionality of man-ufacturing, distribution and finance – the objective being to improve the operation and balance resources.

Enterprise resource planning is a set of integrated software – pro-viding methods of communication between processes and functions across all functions and processes, thereby improving overall data accuracy and decision-making. Enterprise resource planning systems are typically focused on transactional management. It is a modular assessment tool helping to benchmark standards, but does not itself compare modules with modules to gauge planning decisions and their likely effects.

Enterprise resource planning systems are modular in structure and may include: order management, sales forecasts, master planning, BOM data, cost management, maintenance management, human resource management, and so on. The modules are interdependent with specific data collated into a single module which is accessible by other modules or external systems.

Chapter 10
Shop-floor control

One of the objectives for the progressive company is to create a customer-focused orientation within the organization. Each unit or function understands the needs of the end user and deploys those requirements throughout the organization. Each unit then acts as a network of focused problem-solvers. If quality, for example, is an issue for the customer, then the quality assurance system is a network-prioritized activity that plays a role in satisfying the customer.

An integrated shop floor can move the organization forward to becoming a customer-orientated entity in contrast to the traditionally orientated approach, compared in Figure 10.1.

Continuous development of the understanding about the customer–supplier relationship between functions is vital in developing the customer-orientated organization. The flow of work between customer–supplier links is, after all, a communication flow. Measures which appear small can perpetuate the customer–supplier

	Traditional company	Progressive company
Structure	- Form comes first - Central control	- Need comes first - Decentralized control
Organizational responsibility	- Top/staff provides order - Top/staff is responsible	- Top/staff assists the rest - Everybody shares responsibility
Customer orientation	- Crude - At the top/specialist	- More refined - By everybody
Key player		
- Quality - Cost - Delivery	- Inspector, quality staff - Industrial engineer - Expeditor, scheduler	Everybody, including shop-floor people, is involved

Figure 10.1 Comparison of customer orientation between traditional and progressive companies   *Source*: Suzaski (1993).

perspective. Visible charts at workstations (performance indices) are an example of communication flow within the organization. Details about standard operating procedures and work centre activities can be displayed so it becomes clear what takes place where, and when.

Attitudes, motivation and relationships with management are part of the reality of the shop floor (and, indeed, the organization). Finding better ways to do things, progressively, consistently and uniformly requires a new relationship between manager and worker. Figure 10.2 highlights some of consequences of the neglect of proper shop-floor management that stifles participation and helps create a 'them and us' mentality.

The manager should ideally be a facilitator helping to steer the company in the right direction, aided by the worker – a willing par-

Key concerns	Problems
Basic skills are missing, e.g. reading, maths	Someone else has to do the work and rectify the problems. (This may happen if management does not pay any attention to the growth of people and treats people simply as extensions of machines.)
No clear definition of requirements, e.g. inspection standards	Supervisor must be called every time something comes up that is unclear. Time is wasted, and often poor decisions may be made, creating even more problems.
Lack of discipline to follow standards, e.g. housekeeping, workplace organization, work standards	Extra work is created e.g. rework, janitorial work, unnecessary fire-fighting, problem-solving work to identify and correct the situation. Also, the same or similar problems may be repeated over and over again.
Lack of problem-solving skills	Staff, engineers, or managers need to be involved to solve the problem. People's creative talent is not utilized, overhead cost will be increased, and support staff's time will be taken away from more important jobs.
Inflexibility in meeting customers' demands	People cannot cope with changing demands. Self-control ability is missing. This may generate waste in more fire-fighting, additional people, machines, computers, etc.
Inability to cope with frequent introduction of new models	As model change occurs frequently, most of the work has to be done by engineers rather than having detailed work done by people on the shop floor.

Figure 10.2 Problems generated from lack of proper shop-floor management
Source: Suzaski (1993).

ticipant. Facilitation of the worker environment by management can be driven in two distinct ways. One way is to replace employees, including managers, with those who have the current required skills. New blood brings new ideas. The drawback, though, is that the vast majority of the workforce may remain underutilized. A new manager may pull some employees along but a significant element may remain untouched.

The other way is to focus on the entire workforce as one entity and address management of the organization as a motivational issue. How do we get the best from the majority, if not all, of the workforce? Motivational management looks at positive ways to encourage participation by addressing the needs of the workforce, such as stability, enjoyment, responsibility, objectives, equality and identity with the 'team' or organization.

Whatever breaks down the relationship between manager and worker should be addressed (and it might be labelling and stigmatization such as manager/worker classifications). For example, work that has contributed to increased efficiencies in a particular function now means a worker is not required. This worker should be positively encouraged to go on making improvements by being retrained for some other activity with perhaps more responsibility and payment. However motivation management is carried out, the objectives are to facilitate workers' participation and not stifle a valuable resource.

Motivation management should be uniform in approach and not driven by 'easy targets'. It is in many ways counterproductive to have one work centre achieving results of 95 per cent output, and have another that can only manage 70 per cent. Collective output is the measured objective so that the needs of all are understood by motivational management.

Supply chain management will increasingly add to the misery of the traditional manager/worker approach to shop-floor management. Factors such as new technologies, increased product diversity with quicker time to market for product introductions, continuous improvement at greater speed, speed of workflows and information flow requirements will cause much turbulence and stress where managers have to devote far too much time fighting fires, thus perpetuating worker distrust and reaction to chaotic working environments. Figure 10.3 illustrates some of the differences between the traditional approach to shop-floor control and the progressive supply chain management integration approach.

Elements of shop-floor management	Traditional organization	Progressive organization
Core values (Vision)	- Not shared with people - Emphasis on financials	- Shared with people - Emphasis on respect for people
Customer orientation	- Driven by self-interest - Do not understand who the customer is	- Driven to satisfy customers - Next process is the customer
Involvement of everybody	- Labour as extension of machine - Narrow skill base	- Vital element for continuous improvement - Multiple skill base
Problem-solving	- Periodic breakthroughs - Problem-solving by few specialists/professionals	- Continuous improvement - Problem-solving by everyone
Leadership for continuous improvement	- Professional manager - Power-driven	- Leader, educator, catalyst, mentor - People-driven
Management support system	- Centralized planning - Driven by financial result	- Centralized and decentralized planning - Driven by shared values, vision, objectives and means to achieve them

Figure 10.3 Difference between traditional and progressive organizations
Source: Suzaski (1993).

Companies within companies

A company within a company is a cell- or team-based approach. It is an independent unit, but not independent of the organization. The mission and vision of the cell is fundamentally the same as those of the wider organization. The customer–suppler relationship will mechanize the interactions of the group whilst promoting self-management.

A company within a company is a structure within a structure. Reporting structures, expectations and ownership of responsibility are given to each team member. The exact structure of individual responsibility may vary, but should include assigned responsibilities for optimizing the cell, which may include a training representative, safety/housekeeping representative, quality representative, team representative, and so on.

Housekeeping

Any visitor unfamiliar with the shop floor should ideally be able to ask anyone on the shop floor about a particular activity and have their question answered. Good housekeeping is not just a place for everything and everything in its place. Information also requires good housekeeping, such as key performance indicators (KPI), standardized work systems, their organizational structures, procedures, customer–supplier flows, and so on. Good housekeeping is a transparency, where as often as possible the answer is self-explanatory, backed up by an educated workforce. This is not achieved with management slogans, but by participation and identity with processes, objectives and people.

Chapter 11

Purchasing

It has been 'wisely' observed that organizations make profits only when they meet the outside world. Internally, although adding value, costs are part of the product's progress. Evidence would suggest that companies are increasing efficiencies by means of technology utilization, scale and strategy, to increase purchasing content with less direct labour and, thereby, are reducing the value added internally as a proportion of direct labour costs. This trend can be viewed from the differences in the ratios between the degree of purchasing content compared with internal labour content. In the 1980s there was a 3:1 ratio respectively. In the 1990s it was a 4:1 ratio. The trend suggests that the ratio will increase further.

The importance of the purchasing function has traditionally depended both on the ratio mentioned above and the perspectives of management. The importance of the purchasing function can be viewed as a reflection in its hierarchical layout within the organization. Where management considers the purchasing function to be mainly an operational activity, the purchasing department is likely to be placed low down in the organizational hierarchy. Where management view the purchasing function with strategic importance, the reporting levels might include the board of directors.

Traditional definitions of the purchasing function encompasses the process of buying, selecting a supplier, arriving at a price, specifying terms and conditions, issuing a contract or order and expediting delivery. The traditional purchasing function has not typically incorporated supplier-partnering into its strategy. Figure 11.1 compares this traditional perspective with the partnership approach.

The traditional purchasing approach
Advantaged viewpoint
Vendor assessment
Supplier development
Best 'negotiated' price
Adversarial negotiation

Today's partnership approach
Elimination of wasteful practices/duplication
Relationship assessment
Relationship and strategic development
Cost transparency
Collaborative negotiation

Figure 11.1 The traditional purchasing approach compared with the partnership purchasing approach

Web-based purchasing

The web is a communication medium connecting organizations, functions and people around the world. This is in effect an addition to the parallels of the supply chain management ethos – integration and, through integration, visibility. A major inhibitor for purchasing, particularly purchasing spend visibility, is the disaggregation of what is spent on direct and indirect purchasing, how it is spent and the management of the detail about what is received.

Information technology has been used for some time to aid direct purchasing, e.g. MRP II, EDI and, even, e-mail. More can be done, i.e. intranets and extranets, and in particular many gains can be made with indirect purchases. Web-based purchasing systems are a way of realizing the advantages of clarifying and improving the flow and efficiency of the purchasing function(s). Web-based systems can help process transactions, streamlining buying activities from vendors with pre-negotiated deals which means purchases can take place directly from the web without the need to go through the purchasing function, for authorized personnel. Transactions costs are reduced and purchases are made in 'real time'.

Fundamentals of purchasing

The traditional objectives of purchasing at the right price, at the right time and quantity, and obtaining the right quality from the right source still holds true today. However, the detail of the objectives have changed and are continually changing. Each objective is a moving target and no single objective can be left to lag behind the others. Let us consider some of the detail of these objectives.

Right price

A typical manufacturing company spends over 55 per cent of its turnover buying in goods and services. This monetary scale is significant whatever the size of the organization, but is clearly emphasized by large organizations that will spend hundreds of millions, or even billions, of pounds on total purchasing.

It is an important fact for those connected directly or indirectly with the purchasing function that purchasing is not just about buying direct material for the line (direct purchases). Indirect purchasing can account for many millions of pounds of the total spend on areas such as: information technology, training, travel, insurance, energy, facilities, contractors, printing/publishing, office supplies, health care, freight, packaging, and so on. Figure 11.2 clearly illustrates the benefits of reductions in spend for all forms of purchasing activity, whether direct or indirect.

Companies total sales	=	£10,000,000
Purchased services and materials	=	£ 7,000,000
Salaries	=	£ 2,000,000
Overheads	=	£ 500,000
Therefore, Profit	=	£ 500,000

Profits could be doubled to £1 million by any of the following:

Increased sales revenue by 100%
Decrease salaries by 25%
Decrease overheads by 100%
Decrease purchase costs by 7.2%

Figure 11.2 The benefits of reductions in purchasing spend

Right time and quantity

Probably the simplest form of demand communication between customer and supplier is a kanban system. For example, in a three-bin system the customer has two bins on site. One bin might be on the line with the other bin in a backup area. When the bin on the line is emptied, the bin from backup is placed on the line. The fact that the bin on the line is empty is 'automatically' communicated to the supplier who will then send a replacement full bin and work on filling the empty bin from the customer ready for the next call-off. All the activities of replenishment, lead times, packaging requirements and stock location are agreed as part of the system which incorporates self-perpetuating routines and fail-safes.

A JIT system is dependent on very small lot sizes (ideally one) with frequent deliveries and fairly stable demand patterns. The JIT system is dependent on a formal communication system operating as close to real-time demand as possible. The important point about this type of call-off system is that demand is 'real'. Parts are not ordered for stock.

For those parts that are not kanban or JIT scheduled, the likelihood is that a material planner or the MRP system, or a combination of the two, will decide what is required to be ordered, based on safety stock levels, order policies, demand, lead times, and so on. This type of material management would work with ease if the model comprised a simple customer–supplier supply chain with goods flowing in one direction and information flowing in the other direction.

The conflict of low inventory holding, but supply to the customer on time, coupled with demand variability, multifunctional and multiple upstream business links and associated communication time-lags, means that demand changes can result in disproportionate reaction. A chain reaction of nervousness is likely, a result of over-compensation, but may not be recognized as such because a few line item changes here and there over time become lost in the overall developing situation. The cause and effect of demand, quantities and timings become masked.

The effects of demand amplification has become known as the 'Forrester effect' (Forrester, 1961). Figure 11.3 is an example of a simplistic supply chain with information flowing in one direction and material flowing in the other direction, both at the same rate. This balance means the two circles are oscillating at the same speed. Figure 11.4 is an example of a more realistic supply chain comprising multiple business links. In this example a change in demand in business link A could lead business link B to 'anticipate', becoming nervous about demand variability and its ability to offer continuous supply, thereby 'playing safe' by amplifying the demand variation from business link A by disproportinately rescheduling business link C. Likewise, busines link C reschedules business link D, and so on. A fluctuation in demand, even a small gentle vibration, will be amplified until the system becomes virtually uncontrollable.

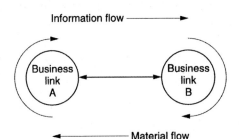

Figure 11.3

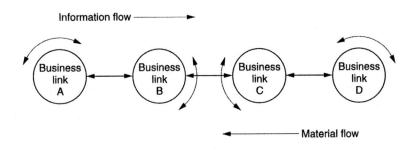

Figure 11.4

Right quality

Quality is fundamental to the whole supply chain. The efficiency of the supply chain can be accelerated or halted by quality. A study carried out in the mid-1990s by the Society of British Aerospace Companies (SBAC, 1996) found that almost half of the sixty respondents inspected 50 per cent of components and 22 per cent inspected every part. It might seem irrelevant to cite an example of a study carried out in the mid-1990s, but the point is that quality concerns and quality inspections have not gone away. Quality is still a key issue at the start of the twenty-first century.

Quality really should not be an issue. If it is an issue, what is the root cause? Quality issues signify some break either in understanding what is required, procedures or attitudes. It procures advancement to JIT systems, lot size reductions and right first time throughput. It strains confidence in relationships and adds cost. Quality, as has been said many times, should be assured. All too often, though, this is projected as an empty slogan when it should be a managed and agreed activity from design, to source, to customer.

Right source

The traditional adversarial customer–supplier relationships have fuelled an arm's length approach between parties. Customers do not want to become too dependent on any one supplier, nor do customers want any one supplier to become too dependent on them. This arm's length approach has led to a multiple sourcing strategy.

Armed with a multiple choice supply base, the purchasing portfolio can play one supplier off against the other in order to achieve the 'best' deal. The sort of terms and the nature of this strategy will drive the customer to look within the supply base for price opportunities wherever possible, which means that periodically the business is put out to re-tender, which could be regardless of excellence of quality and service. In this superficial relationship the supplier looks at each contract on a stand-alone profit basis and makes investments accordingly. During the life of the contract the supplier would be prudent to look for other sources of business from other customers to safeguard continuity of work.

The logic of the traditional customer–supplier relationship suggests that neither party is maximizing its potential. Typically a company will make 80 per cent of its purchases from 20 per cent of its suppliers, therefore, having a small number of key suppliers devoted to long-term relationships can maximize the breath of services it is able to offer, including continuity of supply, quality improvements, costs transparency and improvements, and product development.

Table 11.1 illustrates some of the advantages that Japanese firms have realized by developing relationships with their supply base. From a synopsis of this data we can see advantages include the amount of engineering carried out by Japanese suppliers to customers in Japan – 70 per cent of all components parts. This is a fundamental comparative advantage for the car manufacturer. It helps get new products to the market more quickly and more frequently. Also of note are the differences, particularly with Japanese car manufacturers in Japan supplied by Japanese suppliers, in that they have fewer suppliers, higher levels of JIT supply, less inventory and better quality.

Selecting the right suppliers becomes even more critical where the organizational strategy is to reduce its supply base and thereby deal with a smaller number of selected vendors. It is vital that the reasons for sourcing and supplier selection should follow agreed vendor appraisal criteria. The exact detail of the vendor selection programme might comprise a list of desirable attributes, or only dealing with suppliers who have International Standards Organization (ISO) accreditation, or a complete supplier certification programme, and so on.

	JJ	JA	AA	EE
Engineering carried out by suppliers:				
% of total hours	51.0	n/a	14.0	37.0
% of total parts	70.0	n/a	19.0	46.0
No. of suppliers per assembly plant	170.0	238.0	509.0	442.0
Inventory levels (days)	0.2	1.6	2.9	2.0
Proportion of parts delivered JIT (%)	45.0	35.4	14.8	7.9
Proportion of single-sourced parts (%)	12.1	98.0	69.3	32.9
Quality defects per 100 vehicles (average)	60.0	65.0	82.3	97.0
Average development time per new car (months)	46.2	–	60.4	57.3
Average product life (years)	2.0	–	5.0	5.0
Volume profile, last 20 years	Strong growth	Strong growth	Strong decline	Slight decline

Note: JJ: Japanese companies located in Japan.
JA: Japanese companies located in America.
AA: American companies located in America.
EE: European companies located in Europe.
Source: Womack, Jones and Roos (1990).

Table 11.1 Advantages that Japanese firms have realized by developing relationships with their supply base

The source of supply and reasons for sourcing should be part of the organization's long-term business strategy. For example, take a large multinational company with manufacturing sites around the world with numerous local sources of supply for similar product types. It might be deemed beneficial to consider commodity sourcing, i.e. to have one worldwide source of supply for a particular component type. This could realize major cost savings through scale, and increase research and development potential by dealing with a market-leading supplier in that commodity field, or by helping a supplier to become a leading expert in the field and completely and formally committed to that supply chain – part of the supply chain gameplan.

Chapter 12

Supplier partnering

The concept of supplier partnering is one of mutual dependence, trust and choice. The businesses are viewed as independent but dependent on each other. They share the same values and visions, and communicate as an extended business entity.

Supplier partnering is not something that happens overnight. It is a process developed over time – a long-term commitment. The Japanese have been leaders in recognizing the importance and benefits that a long-term, trusting relationship can offer. Trust is a key ingredient, after all a true partnership is between people and not pieces of paper. Sako (1992) distinguishes trust as:

1 *Contractual trust*: a belief that one party can sue the other for not delivering. A principal over time resulting in more prescriptive and detailed contracts, but used in conjunction with 100 per cent quality inspection.

2 *Competence trust*: a prescriptive contract is still in place, but it is accepted that the other party will behave in a predictable manner – that they are competent at their job. Quality checks will still be carried out.

3 *Goodwill trust*: according to Sako this is the basis of Japanese trading. It is the justified acknowledgement that both parties are on the same side. The supplier will do something because it shares the other party's objectives, and not because it is contracted to do so.

Within the supply chain there will be an operation or key business link which sets the standard for the rest of the supply chain. In an automotive supply chain, for example, the key operation is likely to be the vehicle manufacturing plant even though it is several links upstream in the supply chain. It sets the standards and probably determines the design of the infrastructure.

Supplier partnering should ideally start with the internal philoso-phy of the key operation in the supply chain. Supplier partnering should be an expansion of the ethos which has been developed within the organization, where employees are considered an integral part of the process. Information and successes are shared among employees. Employees who develop trust in the organization can translate that trust to previously antagonistic relationships with suppliers. Employees are better able to partner with outsiders if they have learnt to partner with their fellow employees.

In the product development section we discussed some of the advantages of cross-functional participation in developing new prod-ucts. We have also discussed the advantages of creating a customer-orientated environment. Research carried out by the Institute of Operations Management during 1994 through to 1996 with researchers from Warwick Business School, and with help from oper-ations management associations in France, Germany, Sweden and the Netherlands looked at the spread of technologies for operations man-agement across firms in the manufacturing industry (Robertson, Swan and Newel, 1997). The result of the UK survey, comprising some 4000 Institute of Operations Management members and asking about the adoption and successes of technology initiatives, received 993 responses. Of these 675 were working directly in the manufacturing industry.

The size of the organizations represented by the respondents is shown in Table 12.1. The respondents were asked to rate on a scale of one (not at all successful) to five (very successful) the successes of technologies implemented within their organization. Figure 12.1 shows that, of all the technologies implemented, cell manufacturing was regarded as the most successful. There really should not be any surprise at these results. People working together, responsible, sharing, identifying with objectives and individual and mutual devel-opment is logically a better way of doing things.

Supplier partnering is the application of team-based initiatives between organizations. A true partnership is not just a co-operative agreement where the customer commits to a single supplier for improved service and price. It is the development of joint continuous development teams that look for improvements within the individual companies.

Size	Number (N = 675*)	Percentage
Less than 50 employees	23	3.5
50–100 employees	46	7.0
101–300 employees	181	27.0
301–500 employees	111	16.5
501–1000 employees	144	21.0
1001–5000 employees	115	17.0
More than 5000 employees	54	8.0

Note: * One missing data.
Source: Robertson, Swan and Newel (1997).

Table 12.1 The size of manufacturing firms represented in the survey

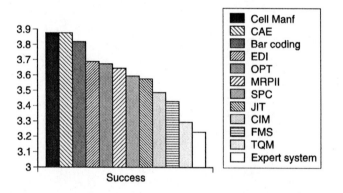

Figure 12.1 Technology success ratings
Source: Robertson, Swan and Newel (1997)

Chapter 13

Logistics

Dictionary definitions of the term logistics includes 'transport' and 'organization of a project'. The actual definition of the application of logistics varies, but essentially it refers to the management of supply chains and incorporates the movement and storage of goods and their associated information flows, from source to customer.

Logistics is a strand running through all the traditional functional aspects of the supply chain from raw material supply, purchasing and manufacturing, to delivery to the customer. The current concept of logistics flows is the integration of time and space – the time materials take to move and the quantity of any material to be moved.

The time and space concept is integrated into the manufacturing environment. Switching to a JIT strategy increases the frequency of deliveries and reduces the amount of material per delivery. A JIT environment is a change in the manufacturing process and material supply, both internally and externally, altering communication flows and the standards of transport service that are required.

The concepts of time and space are key aspects of the logistics system. Current integrated logistics concepts must be responsive to ever increasing market turbulence. The integration of logistics emphasizes the need for companies to remove, or at least alleviate, functional barriers and to focus on streamlined processes designed to meet ever increasing customer and marketplace comparative advantage demands.

Company structures have been developed and are continually being developed to optimize logistics flows, further negating the consequences of fragmentation. Many organizations have appointed logistics directors to realize the potential benefits of strategizing the trade-offs between quality and levels of service and logistics costs.

The appointment of a logistics director is effectively to centralize national and international logistics activities. Centralization of global logistics planning has implications for the way supplies of products and services are structured. Advantages of centralization include advantages of scale of procurement of products and services from the global arena. However, centralization must not impoverish the overall concept of time and space in terms of local market (national markets) competitiveness.

Satisfying 'local' customers within the global arena is a major focus for logistics flows, especially those serious about competing world-wide. Agility or agile logistics is a recognition that centralization brings benefits, but satisfying local customers or markets is a prerequisite. How can this be achieved with local management autonomy without fragmenting the supply chain?

To attempt to answer this we must first distinguish between lean and agile logistics. Lean logistics is about doing more with less. It is often used to describe manufacturing practice which operates effective pull systems, i.e. JIT and kanban, together with other initiatives such as product design and product definition postponement, and so on. The lean environment works well for high-volume, low-variety and predictable markets.

Lean and agile logistics share many fundamental aspects. Product definition postponement is one example. Management of logistics systems along the pipeline and decoupling points (the point at which real demand penetrates the upstream supply chain) from source to the final market is another. To clarify the main differences between the terms 'lean' and 'agile', lean can be thought of as an inbound logistics system. As a result of getting goods into and out of the plant quicker and more efficiently, the goods reach the customer sooner and therefore, one assumes, more competitively.

Agile logistics can be thought of as an outbound logistic system. It primarily addresses the issue of satisfying the customer in the quickest, most efficient way regardless of demand 'certainties' and geography.

Agility is particularly important in satisfying less predictable environments where the demand for variety is high. Agility attempts to effect tailored solutions to demand variability. But it does not stop there. Agility is not some anachronism which can easily be disregarded. It is a logistics perspective that recognizes the need to bring agility into the global marketplace strategy encompassing questions such as: how do we manage the logistics of the global supply chain as well as satisfying local demand? The customer after all expects the same level of performance irrespective of their location.

One way is to outsource logistics to specialists who can offer door-to-door intermodal solutions around the world. Indeed, global logistics specialists can provide networks that allow previously inaccessible markets to be exploited. These benefits can open up the possibility of new service offerings and alternative distribution channels at prices that can stimulate global competitiveness.

Another solution is to time compress the door-to-door logistics flow to the customer. Air transport is one of the world's fastest growing economic sectors. Demand for air freight is expected to grow at 6.6 per cent per year to the year 2015. Given this continued rate of growth the volume of cargo traffic will have tripled by 2015 (Peters and Wright, 1999). Increased product flows with smaller consignment quantities lend themselves to the option of air freight as part of a company's time-elapsed and time-reliability supply chain time-compression strategy.

Sony BPE (Peters and Wright, 1999) is an example of the potential realization of time-compression justification. They source components from Sony, Japan with lengthy lead times given the geographical distances and mode of travel. Table 13.1 shows how they were able to justify defaulting to air freight as a preferred mode of transport.

	Air freight	Sea freight
Administration	2	2
Consolidation	0	5
In-transit	2	28
Booking-in	1	5
Total (days)	5	40
Source: Peters and Wright (1999)		

Table 13.1 Comparison of air freight and sea freight considerations

Air freight reduced lead times by thirty-five days. Additional benefits included reductions in inventory carrying costs. Sony BPE estimates that air freight deliveries will reduce safety stock requirements by 19.6 per cent, leading to an overall reduction in inventory by some 13 per cent. The lessons learnt from compressing time from forty days to five days could be a catalyst for any company to assess all aspects of the

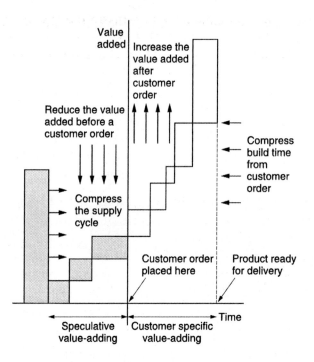

Figure 13.1 A manufacture and logistics repositioning that favours the localization concept   *Source*: Jina (1996).

value chain, first, to measure time for all activities and, then, to address where time is excessive or out of balance, and rectify.

Another solution is to create 'localization' by configuring the product much closer to the point of demand. Figure 13.1 shows a manufacture and logistics repositioning that favours the localization concept. Some speculative value is added before an order is received, but actual definition to a specific customer demand only takes place when a firm order is received. This generic semi-finished global product version could be built centrally and receive localization definition by regional partners.

The localization (agile) concept of product definition postponement differs from the lean logistics perspective. The lean logistics perspective of product definition postponement would likely distribute customers' defined orders from a central point or plant to the specific point of global demand. The agile logistics concept will satisfy the global marketplace by perhaps having a central point or plant which creates a generic product which is shipped out to plants around the world where it is defined by 'local' market demand.

Reverse logistics

A logistics planning system must include reverse logistics, i.e. the return of goods, containers and packaging to the source of supply or distribution. Reusable packaging not only saves time and money, with environmental benefits, it is also required by law. In 1997 the Producer Responsibility Obligations (1997) came into effect (see also University of Westminster, 1998). The aim of the legislation is to place responsibility for packaging recycling on the businesses that either produce or handle packaging. The legislation obligations effect manufacturers, converters, packer/filler, seller, wholesalers and importers.

Standardized and reusable packaging can aid the ergonomic flow of material from inventory storage and on to the production line. Good packaging can help improve warehouse capacity utilization, reduce the need for material handling and can be used as part of the production line ergonomic strategy, including JIT and kanban systems. Reverse logistics is not a hindrance; it is most definitely an opportunity to improve logistics systems.

Chapter 14

Distribution resource planning

Distribution resource planning (DRP) is a process for the management of material requirements for distribution centres. Distribution resource planning can integrate the demands of a number of distribution centres with the source of supply, or a centralized management of supply distribution.

Distribution resource planning, like the MPS, uses a time-phased record. The DRP requirement can be factored into the MPS to show the total distribution demand (Table 14.1). The MPS displays the distribution demands for the product, and the DRP display shows the demand for each product at the distribution centre. This gives the master scheduler the visibility to make decisions about the conflicts of supply and demand with best practice logistics.

	Past due	Week				
		1	2	3	4	5
Distribution demand	200	200	200	250	300	450
Scheduled receipt						
Projected on hand	1200	1000	800	550	250	1000
Master schedule receipt						
Master schedule start			1200			
Notes: Safety stock = 0. Lead time = 3 weeks. Order quantity = 1200.						

Table 14.1 Factoring the DRP requirement into the MPS to show the total distribution demand

The DRP is an extension of information about the total requirements of the netted MPS record. By integrating DRP with the MPS and MRP it is possible to integrate the flow of information across the purchasing, manufacturing and logistics functions. The difference between

DRP and MPS is that in DRP the distribution requirements end at the MPS. In manufacturing everything begins with the MPS.

Chapter 15

Supply chain management checklists

Introduction

The checklists, in an interactive format, are included to help reinforce what has been written in the overview, and therefore should ideally be attempted after completion of the overview.

On completion of the checklists the participant will have a functional and overview perspective of supply chain management. Where improvements in terms of understanding, facilities or procedures have been identified, these can be discussed and prioritized, or they can provide the basis for further development.

How to use the checklists

At the top of most of the pages in the checklists there are two headings. One is 'Understood', the other 'Available'. Below these two headings are two boxes alongside each checklist point (see Figure 15.1 for an example).

The participant should respond in at least one box with a tick for 'yes, understood' or 'yes, available'. If not understood or available, answer with a question mark.

Where a question requires a direct 'yes' or 'no' answer, fill in the 'Understood' box accordingly.

- Understood = participant understands the significance, relevance or answer to the question or point.
- Available = this particular facility or procedure is current practice.

If you have answered the 'Understood' box with a question mark, go back to the overview, or discuss the point with your colleagues, tutor or management.

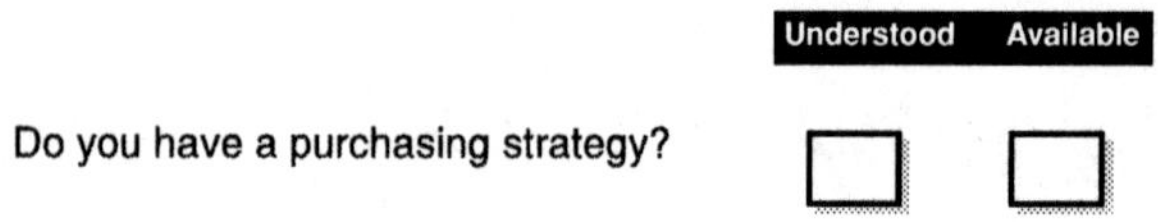

Understood   Available

Do you have a purchasing strategy?   ☐   ☐

Figure 15.1 Example of checklist boxes

If you have answered with 'no' in the 'Understood' box, discuss the point with your colleagues, tutor or management.

If you reply to the 'Understood' box with a tick, but reply with a question mark to 'Available', this should be investigated, discussed or considered for future implementation.

Chapter 16

Checklist: Chapter 1

Understanding the customer

	Understood	Available

Customer profiles are kept on a database (significant background data is compiled about the customer which includes end users and key delivery partners). The profile comprises information on:

	Understood	Available
Customer expectations and desires from the total value package.	☐	☐
Expectations about commitments from the company.	☐	☐
The customer profile database is audited by periodic review to gauge accuracy (this should indicate 99–100 per cent accuracy).	☐	☐
Orders and order patterns are reviewed in order to further understand the customers (and analysis is shared with supply partners).	☐	☐
A programme of customer meetings is in place which is regular and scheduled around customer convenience.	☐	☐
The percentage of customers visited and the scheduled visits targets are measured for audit assessment and proactive analysis.	☐	☐
A system is in place for tracking feedback, both positive and negative, from customers.	☐	☐
The feedback received is shared throughout the organization or where particular feedback is deemed appropriate.	☐	☐

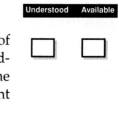

Feedback information is reviewed for frequency of
updates, the effectiveness of communicating feedback to the appropriate people, and whether the
feedback has been actively used for improvement
work.

Upper management is obliged during the year to
spend time in customer services to understand customer experiences and levels of service received.

Customer satisfaction measurement

<table>
<tr><td></td><td>Understood</td><td>Available</td></tr>
<tr><td>A documented working process is in place to measure customer satisfaction.</td><td>☐</td><td>☐</td></tr>
<tr><td>The customer satisfaction measurement is consistently collated and reviewed regularly to monitor customers' perceptions of service.</td><td>☐</td><td>☐</td></tr>
<tr><td>Measurement of customer service indicates continuous improvement in the customer service function.</td><td>☐</td><td>☐</td></tr>
<tr><td>A regular and documented programme of customer meetings is in place, either by phone or in person, which are convenient to the customer (reinforcing/developing relationships).</td><td>☐</td><td>☐</td></tr>
<tr><td>The number of customer requests denied is measured by period (a decline is evidence of increased responsiveness to customer requests).</td><td>☐</td><td>☐</td></tr>
<tr><td>Evidence is available for improved response times to customer enquiries through improved information tools availability (i.e. speed to answer telephone calls, fax, e-mail response times, real-time product availability information, etc.).</td><td>☐</td><td>☐</td></tr>
</table>

Retaining the customer

	Understood	Available

Customer service employees understand what is meant by the definition 'pleasant surprises'. ☐ ☐

There is a documented plan for assuring that customers experience 'pleasant surprises', and evidence is available of plan execution. ☐ ☐

Information is shared with customers via newsletters, reports, etc., which emphasize positive news or key events. ☐ ☐

Customer service employees are part of the strategy and active participants in retaining customers for life. ☐ ☐

Customer service employees proactively share customer information, educating others in the organization about the needs of the customer. ☐ ☐

Capable people

	Understood	Available

Reinforcement of good customer service practice is documented and visible for all employees to see and to practise.

A documented training matrix exists for all customer service personnel.

Each employee participates in a programme of education and problem-solving activities to improve the service to the end and internal customer.

Each customer service employee is trained to use, and have readily available, databases (relational) that enable accurate and timely responses to be given to the customer.

Verification programmes indicate the levels of customer service employees' understanding of key processes that help to serve the customer.

A documented training programme is in place for all new employees to ensure that customer service is not affected by new employee 'learning curves'.

A backup policy exists to support the customer when employees are absent for whatever reason.

The backup policy also includes an information list which is communicated to the customer so that the customer knows whom to contact in the event that the usual contact is unavailable.

Chapter 17

Checklist: Chapter 2

Manufacturing (historical perspective)

Understood   Available

The objectives below are taken from Henry Ford's book, *Today and Tomorrow*, (Ford, 1926). It offers an interesting perspective on some seventy years' 'progress'.

Satisfy customers completely.

Earn adequate profits.

Use capital effectively.

Generate more wealth.

Reward participants equitably.

Treat suppliers and customers fairly.

Be a good citizen.

Managed manufacturing

Understood   Available

Essentially the manufacturing environment is the managed flow of information and materials. Looking at your organization, gauge how well (you) manage information and materials.

Does your organization make promises to customers that are not kept? ☐ ☐

Is the culture of the organization predominantly one of functional inverted perspectives? ☐ ☐

Are problems generally resolved at the root cause? ☐ ☐

Are new product designs completed on time? ☐ ☐

Is quality still a problem for your organization? ☐ ☐

Is machinery effectively utilized? ☐ ☐

Do materials lurch through the plant or do they flow smoothly? ☐ ☐

Do new customer orders or changes come as a surprise to many in the organization? ☐ ☐

Does the organization meet its profit goals? ☐ ☐

Could the goals for profit be improved? ☐ ☐

Information flows

	Understood	Available
Map all information pathways.	☐	☐
Enlist and educate everyone in the organization about the needs of information flow and identify where breaks occur.	☐	☐
Make corrections quickly and make them permanent.	☐	☐
Good planning requires good analysis that can distinguish between problems and symptoms.	☐	☐
Data has to be believed – it needs to be accurate.	☐	☐

Improving the resource of time

	Understood	Available
Time-related focus on improving current activities.	☐	☐
Be intolerant of delays and fix the causes.	☐	☐
Eliminate processes and routines that cushion against time.	☐	☐
Reduce cycle times, but do so for all processes and routines.	☐	☐
The importance of reductions in time for all processes and routines are communicated, measured and rewarded when achieved.	☐	☐

Manufacturing cycle time reduction

Understood   Available

Use the form in Figure 17.1 to measure (it does not have to be exact) how long each event takes and discuss how this could be improved.

☐   ☐

Activity	Days required	Fat days/hours
Order entry		
Release to production		
Production throughput		
Material procurement/receiving		
Incoming inspection		
Raw material storage duration		
Component storage duration		
Kitting components for production		
Final assembly		
Test and repair		
Packaging		
Finished goods stores		
Delivery		
Invoicing		

Note: The fat days/hours column is the cycle time where no value is added. For example the length of time material is sitting idle waiting for processing, or the time it takes to procure a part from ordering, chasing, delivery and quality auditing.

Figure 17.1 Manufacturing cycle time reduction form

Develop your own forms for a specific function or area for improvement for information and material flow.

☐   ☐

Information systems appraisal

Understood   Available

In this checklist you are invited briefly to appraise your own organization's standard of integrated and managed information flows and routines between the customer (next external link) and supplier.

How does your organization typically receive information from the customer:

About demand?

About customer satisfaction?

How is this integrated with:

The product delivery cycle?

Your supply partners?

Using key performance indicators (i.e. order cycle times, on time shipment to the customer), evaluate areas where integration of processes and information sharing could be improved:

From customer to supplier?

From supplier to customer?

Chapter 18

Checklist: Chapter 3

E-commerce strategy assessment

	Understood	Available

E-commerce has the potential fundamentally to reshape the competitive environment. It therefore requires addressing at a strategic level.

	Understood	Available
Vision the effects e-commerce could have on your supply chain model.	☐	☐
Assess the implications of the Internet forum on:		
Customer interaction/expectations.	☐	☐
Your organizational structure.	☐	☐
Your suppliers and their suppliers.	☐	☐
The marketplace – domestic and global.	☐	☐
Distribution channels.	☐	☐
Opportunities/necessities for business integration.	☐	☐
Assess what opportunities are available for improving your supply chain right now.	☐	☐

E-commerce business drivers

	Understood	Available
Enhances potential value creation of the supply chain model.	☐	☐
Innovation in business.	☐	☐
Empowerment of employees.	☐	☐
Cost reductions throughout the supply chain.	☐	☐
Global forum.	☐	☐
Competitive necessity.	☐	☐

E-commerce and your business

	Understood	Available

Does your organization have a web site? ☐ ☐

Do your competitors have a web site? ☐ ☐

Is your/competitor's web site interactive, providing on-line:

Order enquiries/availability? ☐ ☐

Order placement? ☐ ☐

Customer request configuration? ☐ ☐

Price information? ☐ ☐

Order tracking? ☐ ☐

Technical diagnostics/after-sales support? ☐ ☐

On-line implications

	Understood	Available

Global market forum.

Always open to the public.

Compete within national/international markets.

Global distribution channels.

Product configuration for specific markets/countries.

Flexible/demand management optimization.

On-line opportunities

	Understood	Available

Data availability/visibility/modelling.

Data availability for demand patterns.

Data availability for competitor benchmarking.

Value chain development – closer to the customer.

Chapter 19

Checklist: Chapter 4

Product development overview

	Understood	Available
Who is assigned responsibility for approving new product development?	☐	☐
Who manages the product development process?	☐	☐
Does your organization measure product development cycle times?	☐	☐
Is the development cycle time taken from the first activity of development to stable supply of the product in volume to the customer?	☐	☐
Does your organization have a cross-functional development team?	☐	☐

Does your organization typically develop products by:

	Understood	Available
Small steps?	☐	☐
Complete new product introductions?	☐	☐
New product introductions (complete product or product enhancements) are benchmarked for assessment of first to market innovation.	☐	☐

Product change opportunities entail looking outside the organization's own environment and:

	Understood	Available
Taking advantage of unexpected markets.	☐	☐
Changes within the market structure.	☐	☐

	Understood	Available

Changes bought about by social change. ☐ ☐

Technological changes. ☐ ☐

New product development includes consideration of total costs such as:

Quality issues. ☐ ☐

Failures in the field. ☐ ☐

Late deliveries at introduction stages. ☐ ☐

Instability of product design after launch. ☐ ☐

Effects on market goodwill. ☐ ☐

Determination to be 'first to market' requires a broad vision from the board of directors and throughout the organization about where the business is now and where it is going. ☐ ☐

Determination to be 'first to market' requires an overall structure and style that is responsive to product change opportunities and able to exploit them. ☐ ☐

Product development management

	Understood	Available

Product development includes cross-functional integration and vendor participation if required, at least during critical design stages. ☐ ☐

There is assigned product management responsibility linking the functions of:

Design. ☐ ☐

Supply feasibility/procurement. ☐ ☐

Manufacturability. ☐ ☐

Engineering change management. ☐ ☐

Data cleansing/management. ☐ ☐

Field testing. ☐ ☐

After service. ☐ ☐

Production readiness. ☐ ☐

Product development schedules outline objectives, timescales and budgets. ☐ ☐

Product development schedules include analysis of cycle times, on time completion and reports on improvement possibilities. ☐ ☐

Product development time frames are realistic and are used for sales planning and master production scheduling planning. ☐ ☐

Product design wherever possible should factor commonality of components with existing designs. ☐ ☐

'Tweaks' to designs and larger product developments require available capacity for speedy conclusion of objectives. This should be a known and factored variable parameter. ☐ ☐

	Understood	Available

Sufficient capacity is available to encourage proactive product improvements driven by customers, marketing, manufacturing, quality and suppliers. □ □

Individual engineering changes are considered as part of the overall development strategy. □ □

Product development improvement opportunities

Understood   Available

Could the product be improved by addressing:

Current cycle time development. ☐ ☐

Small stages improvements. ☐ ☐

Application of product function. ☐ ☐

Degree of justifiable variety. ☐ ☐

Reliability. ☐ ☐

Maintenance. ☐ ☐

Price. ☐ ☐

After-sales support (including use of information technology systems for monitoring/fault diagnosis/support). ☐ ☐

Warranty costs. ☐ ☐

Global product design

Understood   Available

Is there a core manufacturability of your product which would not be affected by demand variations?   ☐   ☐

Could a core configuration of manufacture be cost-justified without hindrance to customer lead times?   ☐   ☐

Are the benefits of modular configuration considered in design, which include:

Manufacturing (modular commitment at latest stages of process manufacture)?   ☐   ☐

After-service (replacement module for module)?   ☐   ☐

Order configuration (easier for customers to select a module by module make-up of their requirements)?   ☐   ☐

Reliability (quality issues analysis by module)?   ☐   ☐

Chapter 20

Checklist: Chapter 5

The mass customization journey

	Understood	Available

Look at the market turbulence factors mapped in Figure 20.1 and consider the following questions:

Is your market environment less turbulent than five years ago? ☐ ☐

Is your market environment the same? ☐ ☐

Is your market environment more turbulent than five years ago? ☐ ☐

Assess the scale of change – determine the vision (Pine, 1993) ☐ ☐

Organizing for mass customization

	Understood	Available

Development: cycle time reductions for development. ☐ ☐

Production: cycle time reductions for production. ☐ ☐

Marketing: market mass customization as a standard service. ☐ ☐

Delivery: deliver globally what the customer wants at local market speed. ☐ ☐

Who	• Who needs my product/service? • What about it is inherently personal so that it can differ for each individual? • How do my customers differ? • How can I satisfy whoever wants my product/service?
What	• What do customers do differently with my product/service? • What different forms can it take? • How can I satisfy whatever customers want from my product/service?
Where	• Where do customers need my product/service? • How do customers differ in where they buy, receive and use it? • How can I provide my product/service wherever customers want it?
When	• When do customers need my product/service? • How do customers differ in when they buy, receive and use it? • How can I provide my product/service twenty-four hours a day? • How can I provide my product/service the instant customers want it? • How can I provide my product/service whenever customers want it?
Why	• Why do customers need my product/service? • How do customers differ in why they buy, receive and use it? • Is my product/service a means or an end, or something in between? • How can I add more value to help my customers completely meet their true desired end?
How	• How do customers need my product/service delivered to them? • How do customers differ in how they buy and use it? • What can I do to provide my product/service however my customers want it?

Figure 20.1 Market turbulence factors

Source: Adapted from Pine (1993).

Determining strategy – incorporating mass customization

	Understood	Available

Scenario planning: model and gauge alternative futures for your organization in the changing marketplace.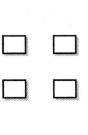

Envisage the best responses to each alternative scenario.

Strategy encompasses the firm's current standing, coupled with a structure for change.

The strategies themselves must be flexible and readily address rapid environmental changes, which include:

Products.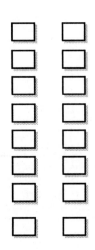

Markets (global).

Technologies.

Life cycles.

Competition.

Financials.

Economics.

Within the mass customized global environment a strategy cycle is how often, how fast, and the speed of responses that must be made to the firm's changing environment.

Whatever the strategy cycles, the consistency of purpose and clarity of vision remain the constant theme.

The strategies include the synergy between thinking and doing – if top management define the broad strategic intent, then the does at all levels determine the best strategic actions for implementation.

Customizing standard products and services (Pine, 1993)

	Understood	Available

Development: continue to develop a standard product or service. ☐ ☐

Production: continue to produce the standard product or service. ☐ ☐

Marketing: use the standard product or service but find ways to customize it in the market. ☐ ☐

Delivery: deliver a customized service as well as a standard service for the product or service ☐ ☐

Customizing the product or service (Pine, 1993)

	Understood	Available
Development: develop a product or service which is customizable.	☐	☐
Production: produce a standard or core product or service which can be customized.	☐	☐
Marketing: market the customizable benefits to the marketplace.	☐	☐
Delivery: take the standard product or service and find ways to customize its delivery.	☐	☐

Customizing the point of delivery (Pine, 1993)

	Understood	Available

Development: use the standard product or service. ☐ ☐

Production: produce the product or service in a central location in a standard format. ☐ ☐

Marketing: market the product or service as mass customized. ☐ ☐

Delivery: deliver a standard product which can be mass customized. ☐ ☐

Moving production closer to the customer (Pine, 1993)

	Understood	Available
Development: develop products or services that can be delivered mass customized to the customer.	☐	☐
Marketing: market the mass customized benefits.	☐	☐
Production: produce a mass customized product or service.	☐	☐
Delivery: deliver a mass customized product or service.	☐	☐

Chapter 21

Checklist: Chapter 6

Forecasting made easier

	Understood	Available
Balance the flow between total supply lead time and supply chain cycle times.	☐	☐
Product design/definition: define the product at the latest possible stage and as close as possible to point of real demand.	☐	☐
Integrate and optimize inventory flows, i.e. JIT, kanban, third party warehousing.	☐	☐
Reduce manufacturing lead times.	☐	☐
Professionally collated forecasts utilizing market intelligence from marketing/sales functions.	☐	☐
Forecast by product family.	☐	☐
Easy to understand, transparent forecast formulation.	☐	☐
Focus on forecast accuracy performance – continuous measurement/alignment.	☐	☐
Pareto 80:20 rule – 20 per cent of the forecast will cover 80 per cent of the total demand. Increase attention on the 20 per cent and leave the 80 per cent to the computer.	☐	☐
Forecast with the customer – customer profile assimilation.	☐	☐

Forecasting using information technology

	Understood	Available

Is there assigned responsibility for developing and maintaining forecasts? ☐ ☐

Can forecast accuracy be measured by:

Volume? ☐ ☐

Mix? ☐ ☐

Part number? ☐ ☐

Can variance reports for previous forecasts be produced? ☐ ☐

Are original and revised forecasts maintained? ☐ ☐

Are sales tracked to forecast? ☐ ☐

Is there a selection of 'best fit' forecasting techniques available? ☐ ☐

Can comments be added to forecast reports and viewed on line? ☐ ☐

Can a forecast be created by:

Specification level? ☐ ☐

Model? ☐ ☐

Family? ☐ ☐

Customer? ☐ ☐

Other? ☐ ☐

Can specified items be identified as 'manual' forecast only? ☐ ☐

Can 'new product' forecasts be frozen for a user-defined period? ☐ ☐

	Understood	Available

Are forecasts possible for defined multidimensional ABC classifications (pareto 80:20 rule)? ☐ ☐

Does the forecast system allow input of market knowledge related information? ☐ ☐

Is there an EDI facility or system-integrated procedure for communicating forecasts with upstream supply partners? ☐ ☐

Forecasting: supply considerations

	Understood	Available

Supply constraints analysis. ☐ ☐

Logistics modelling: inventory location modelling – develop the value chain. ☐ ☐

Supplier relationship/communication – 'joint effort' mind-set. ☐ ☐

Seasonal analysis – capacity levelling. ☐ ☐

EDI scheduling – real-time information-sharing commitments. ☐ ☐

Forecasting: demand considerations

Understood   Available

(See also, demand management.)

Accurate communication of demand and availability is forwarded to all trading partners. ☐ ☐

Current and projected demand is managed. ☐ ☐

Measurement standards for demand management processes. ☐ ☐

Demand fulfilment is conducive with business goals and objectives. ☐ ☐

Demand management is structured into and measured into the overall performance of the organization. ☐ ☐

Forecasting: potential performance benefits

	Understood	Available
Improved customer service.	☐	☐
Reduced manufacturing inefficiencies.	☐	☐
Improved manufacturing/sales communication.	☐	☐
System compiled analysis.	☐	☐
Fewer back orders.	☐	☐
Reduced lost sales.	☐	☐
Improved production planning.	☐	☐
Reduced expediting costs (unanticipated demand).	☐	☐
Fewer stock-outs.	☐	☐
Reduced inventory levels/better inventory control.	☐	☐
Improved direct labour productivity.	☐	☐
Focused effort on exceptions for immediate action.	☐	☐
Better budgeting.	☐	☐
Increased revenue growth.	☐	☐
Cycle time reductions.	☐	☐
More stable supplier scheduling.	☐	☐
Less added costs/reduction in waste.	☐	☐

Chapter 22

Checklist: Chapter 7

Customer order management

	Understood	Available

Processes are in place which document the number of customer requests denied (such denials drive process reviews of internal processes to streamline and make 'friendly' the customer order management process). ☐ ☐

Communication systems are in place (such as telephones, faxes, e-mail, etc.) which allow prompt and professional handling of enquiries. ☐ ☐

Customer service personnel have ready access to documented concise information to key processes which help give good customer service. ☐ ☐

Customer service processes are documented, visible and effective. ☐ ☐

Benchmark visits are utilized to identify 'best practices' continually to improve processes. ☐ ☐

Orders are received and acknowledged in the shortest possible time, consistently. Ideally real-time receipt/acknowledgement is the goal. ☐ ☐

Guidelines are in place to ensure prompt responses to both enquiries and new product orders. ☐ ☐

Order entry accuracy is measured and targets/objectives are defined. ☐ ☐

	Understood	Available

Discrepancies are resolved, or at least resolution of an issue is closed from the customer perspective, promptly and within specified measured parameters. ☐ ☐

A downward trend is evident in the cycle times to reply to customer orders and enquiries. ☐ ☐

The customer order management service allows the customer to communicate in his or her own language (i.e. if the customer prefers to speak German, the service should have the capacity to communicate in German. Or the customer is able communicate using his part numbers). ☐ ☐

Processes are regularly audited to ensure that the customer is receiving a consistent service. ☐ ☐

A documented process is in place, with evidence of adherence, which provides a prompt resolution for discrepancies (i.e. shipping errors, quality issues, late deliveries, documentation issues). ☐ ☐

Customer on-time delivery information is measured, tracked and benchmarked against customer service levels, and shared with customers, managers and the wider organization. ☐ ☐

Chapter 23
Checklist: Chapter 8

Demand management principal objectives

	Understood	Available
Manage demand for effective and cost-efficient utilization of resources and integrity of order promising.	☐	☐
Customer service standards are known, communicated internally and externally, managed and developed.	☐	☐
Order promising and inbound and outbound production flow must be co-ordinated through a master production schedule system.	☐	☐
Order promising must be done using available to promise concepts.	☐	☐
Management of demand must capture all sources of demand and properly identify order timings, quantity and location.	☐	☐
Forecast inaccuracy is inevitable. Management attention must give weighted focus to responsiveness of actual demand conditions.	☐	☐

Defining customer expectations

Understood   Available

Marketing and manufacturing should work
together to define:

Response times.   ☐   ☐

Order sizes.   ☐   ☐

Order frequency.   ☐   ☐

Packaging requirements.   ☐   ☐

Shipping modes.   ☐   ☐

Demand management measurement and review

Understood   Available

(Your company appraisal.)

What are realistic customer delivery aims:

When the customer states they want the
product?   ☐   ☐

Order acknowledgement date given when the
order was placed?   ☐   ☐

When the customer wants to use the product
(but has bought ahead)?   ☐   ☐

When the customer ideally wants to use the
product?   ☐   ☐

Delivery fulfilment ex-works?   ☐   ☐

Delivery fulfilment shipped to the customer?   ☐   ☐

Satisfying demand: your company interpretation

	Understood	Available
Shipment of the whole order?	☐	☐
A quantity of the product line?	☐	☐
The full quantity of the product line?	☐	☐
A balanced fulfilment of the order?	☐	☐

Satisfying demand: lead time measurement at your company

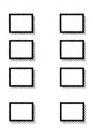

Understood   Available

Demand is satisfied within:

X hours.

X days.

X weeks.

Does this vary depending on the product/customer?

Measuring order fulfilment/service levels

Understood   Available

Collect performance data from the checklists on
pages 129–131 for order fulfilment measurement.
Order fulfilment should select the best fit for the
'average' customer (objective is to consistently
measure performance/trends).

$$\% \text{ order fulfilment} = \frac{\text{demand satisfied} \times 100}{\text{total demand}}$$

Demand capacity: sales and marketing

	Understood	Available

Actual sales are measured against the sales plan. ☐ ☐

The system of compensation for sales achievement should not affect the formulation of sales planning and forecasting. ☐ ☐

The pursuance of sales and customer linking into the planning system will help communicate and alleviate demand variance. ☐ ☐

The need for time fences is understood and agreed by sales and marketing and manufacturing. ☐ ☐

Time fences are periodically reviewed. The objective is to reduce firm time fences for managing change. ☐ ☐

Time fences should only be changed if they can be consistently managed, maintaining order-promising integrity and profitability. ☐ ☐

Chapter 24

Checklist: Chapter 9

Master production schedule

	Understood	Available
The master production schedule is a 'funnel' through which the details about demand are drawn together, sifted and, as near as possible, balanced by supply.	☐	☐
Responsibility for the activities of maintaining the master production schedule is clearly assigned.	☐	☐
The importance of this position is reflected within the management structure and reporting relationships.	☐	☐
Master production planning is a dynamic process that requires understanding of the products, the manufacturing process and the manufacturing planning and control system.	☐	☐
The master production schedule makes available information to the customer which reliably (given known variables) gives available-to-promise information.	☐	☐
The master scheduler is part of the communication channel which advises on capacity or material problems so that contingency and resolution planning can be effected.	☐	☐
The master scheduler must keep the parts (master production schedule) equal to the whole (production plan).	☐	☐

	Understood	Available

The master production schedule is aligned to the agreed-to-rate of manufacturing output. ☐ ☐

All levels of items are identified and master production scheduled. ☐ ☐

A rough-cut capacity facility is available which can readily evaluate the impact of significant change enquiries on the master production schedule (this should use demonstrated average capacity matrixes for comparison with required capacity implications). ☐ ☐

The master scheduler is a vital link between the process of sales requirements and operations planning and, as such, is the 'level-headed mediator' between the dynamics of demand (sales planning) and supply (operations planning). ☐ ☐

Targets about master production schedule commitments, responsiveness and stability are known policy objectives and are measured by review. ☐ ☐

The master production schedule will require replanning. Frequency of replanning will depend on planning horizons (time-fences), variability of demand, responsiveness and stability objectives. ☐ ☐

Master production schedule changes which occur within the firm period time-fences should be collated and reviewed for cause analysis. ☐ ☐

Consumption of the forecast will alleviate planning nervousness through understanding and transparency of incoming orders. ☐ ☐

The more responsive the master production schedule can be, the closer the needs of demand can be aligned to the ability to supply. ☐ ☐

The master production schedule unit should reflect the company's approach to the environment in which it operates. ☐ ☐

Understood   Available

The master production schedule should be evaluated for performance against clearly defined parameters which reflect the business objectives of the organization.

Capacity

Capacity management is a balance between load and capacity. ☐ ☐

Capacity resource planning addresses what resources are required, how much resource is required and when the resource is required. ☐ ☐

All sources of demand are considered in developing the capacity plan. ☐ ☐

Consideration, where appropriate, is given to engineering and vendor capacity as an extension of the capacity management process. ☐ ☐

Capacity is demonstrated and continually measured against planned versus actual inputs and outputs. ☐ ☐

Data are collated about overload and underload capacity scheduling, and considered for possible corrective action.

Capacity balancing either means addressing bottleneck root causes or it means a strategic loss of capacity in favour of flexibility to react to changes in market conditions. ☐ ☐

Capacity can be measured as:

Time available (this is the time worked compared with the time allowed). ☐ ☐

Productive time (this is the time recorded by the shop floor as allocated to jobs). ☐ ☐

Standard time (total units produced × standard unit times). This is the rate of production that can be expected under normal conditions (a measure of an average operator under average conditions). ☐ ☐

Load is a measure of:

Number of repetitions of the process × times required for each operation + set-up time

Bill of materials

	Understood	Available

Responsibility is determined for developing and maintaining bills of materials. ☐ ☐

Efforts to reduce the number of part numbers are ongoing in order to standardize requirements wherever possible. ☐ ☐

Bills of materials are reviewed for opportunities to make them flatter and thereby reduce lead times (JIT/assembly environment). ☐ ☐

Phasing in and phasing out of bill of material structures should be done in a cost-effective way and consider:

Current stock and work in process. ☐ ☐

After-market replenishment requirements. ☐ ☐

Availability of material, resources and skills. ☐ ☐

Enterprise resource planning (ERP) potential benefits

Improved visibility and management of information. ☐   ☐

Improved quality of data with multi-site comparisons. ☐   ☐

Improved costing assessment. ☐   ☐

Reductions in inventory. ☐   ☐

Improved capacity utilization. ☐   ☐

Purchase cost reductions. ☐   ☐

Reductions in likelihood of material shortages. ☐   ☐

Chapter 25

Checklist: Chapter 10

Rethinking the importance of the shop floor (Suzaski, 1993)

	Understood	Available
Shop-floor activities are crucial to the organization's success.	☐	☐
People engaged in shop-floor activities represent a majority of working people in our society.	☐	☐
People on the shop floor are not only producers of value to society but also customers.	☐	☐
The shop floor provides a critical environment for people's career development.	☐	☐
Many people spend the majority of their working careers on the shop floor.	☐	☐
Developing self-managing capability on the shop floor will help people to chart a course in the current turbulent business environment.	☐	☐

Visual aids for enhanced communication (Suzaski, 1993)

	Understood	Available

Awards: these represent the memory of hard work, or milestones of progress. ☐ ☐

Banners with important messages or slogans remind people of shared beliefs. ☐ ☐

Improvement boards describe through pictures and comments changes made. ☐ ☐

Cross-training charts, skills matrixes, show the skill base of each team member. ☐ ☐

Charts on attendance and number of suggestions help indicate the health of the organization. ☐ ☐

Newsletters recognize improvements and ideas and share company objectives. ☐ ☐

Major features of team improvement activities (Suzaski, 1993)

	Understood	Available
The team is composed mainly of people from the same work area.	☐	☐
The focus is on improving problems on the shop floor.	☐	☐
The emphasis is on self-management and the use of the team's collective wisdom.	☐	☐
Support and guidance may be given by management.	☐	☐
The team contributes to the company's mission as well as their own.	☐	☐
The team explores everyone's creativity and self-esteem.	☐	☐
The team makes use of problem-solving tools.	☐	☐
The team functions continually, aiming for continuous improvement while involving everyone.	☐	☐
The team values individuals and helps through motivation and training to develop their creativity.	☐	☐

Benefits of a company within a company (Suzaski, 1993)

	Understood	Available

People develop a sense of ownership.   ☐ ☐

By focusing on certain subjects as a group, they work better as a team.   ☐ ☐

Developing missions etc. will help members focus on clear objectives.   ☐ ☐

By practising the customer orientation and sharing the processes of developing a business plan and progress report, barriers will be reduced between units of the organization.   ☐ ☐

Chapter 26

Checklist: Chapter 11

Purchasing strategy: suggestions

	Understood	Available
Partnership contribution to business planning, build partnerships with suppliers, in the short and long term.	☐	☐
Purchasing for the right quality, with the right delivery terms at the lowest overall cost.	☐	☐
Search new markets for new and improved products/services.	☐	☐
Develop a continuous development framework for the customer–supplier relationship.	☐	☐

Setting purchasing priorities

	Understood	Available

Bottleneck items:

Ensure continuous supply, if necessary at premium cost. ☐ ☐

Good forecasting and backup plans required. ☐ ☐

Good inventory data required. ☐ ☐

Proactive communication with suppliers. ☐ ☐

Develop strategy for resolving bottlenecks. ☐ ☐

Strategic items:

Good, detailed forecasts. ☐ ☐

Long-term supply relationship development. ☐ ☐

Make v. buy decisions. ☐ ☐

Risk analysis. ☐ ☐

Contingency planning. ☐ ☐

Logistics, inventory and vendor control. ☐ ☐

Non-critical items:

Standardized products. ☐ ☐

Order volume optimization. ☐ ☐

Efficient order processing. ☐ ☐

Inventory optimization. ☐ ☐

Leverage items:

Exploit purchasing power/scale. ☐ ☐

Market/order volume optimization. ☐ ☐

Targeted pricing strategies. ☐ ☐

Indirect cost appraisal/disaggregation

Understood   **Available**

Identify current costs of the following:

	Understood	Available
Information technology.	☐	☐
Training.	☐	☐
Travel.	☐	☐
Insurance.	☐	☐
Energy.	☐	☐
Facilities.	☐	☐
Contractors.	☐	☐
Printing/publishing.	☐	☐
Office supplies.	☐	☐
Freight.	☐	☐
Packaging.	☐	☐

Make v. buy decisions

	Understood	Available

The make or buy decision is part of the strategy towards world-class manufacturing. ☐ ☐

Will a buy decision have less cost with equal or greater quality/reliability? ☐ ☐

Will a buy decision maintain or improve flexibility and responsiveness of in-house capacity and the supply chain? ☐ ☐

A make v. buy decision will consider:

Advantages now. ☐ ☐

Advantages in the future. ☐ ☐

Technology trends. ☐ ☐

Investment implications. ☐ ☐

Health of supply base. ☐ ☐

Future supplies. ☐ ☐

Consideration is given to the effects on:

Marketing. ☐ ☐

Design. ☐ ☐

Personnel. ☐ ☐

Finance. ☐ ☐

Manufacturing. ☐ ☐

Strategic risk assessment criteria

	Understood	Available
Key/critical parts.	☐	☐
Key/critical processes.	☐	☐
Parts over a particular value.	☐	☐
All production parts.	☐	☐
All suppliers.	☐	☐
A supplier.	☐	☐

Reducing your supply base: examples

	Understood	Available
Make v. buy.	☐	☐
Resourcing/partnership sourcing strategies.	☐	☐
Commodity sourcing strategies.	☐	☐
Third party purchasing.	☐	☐
Tiering.	☐	☐
Stockists.	☐	☐

Supply base reduction benefit assessment

	Understood	Available
Quality.	☐	☐
Delivery.	☐	☐
Unit cost/ total cost.	☐	☐
Operating cost.	☐	☐
Lead time reductions.	☐	☐
Technical interface.	☐	☐
Breadth of services development.	☐	☐
Closer relationship.	☐	☐

What criteria are used to approve new suppliers?

	Understood	Available
Capability.	☐	☐
Capacity.	☐	☐
Quality systems.	☐	☐
Financial status.	☐	☐
Product specific.	☐	☐
Process specific.	☐	☐
Business management.	☐	☐
Customer approval.	☐	☐
Third party approval.	☐	☐
Lowest unit cost.	☐	☐
Lowest total cost.	☐	☐
Supplier expertise.	☐	☐
Scale.	☐	☐
Technological.	☐	☐
Other.	☐	☐

Right source appraisal

	Understood	Available

Do new/existing suppliers fulfil the following criteria:

Do they have the ability to carry out the work required? ☐ ☐

Have they the capacity now and for any future anticipated demands? ☐ ☐

Does the supplier understand what is expected of them? ☐ ☐

Is the supplier easy to deal with? ☐ ☐

Are they financially stable? ☐ ☐

Do they have strategies for improvement? ☐ ☐

Vendor rating

Understood   Available

(A guide for reviewing your supply base.)

Quality achievement.

☐ ☐

Deliveries on time.

☐ ☐

Price.

☐ ☐

Co-operation in design.

☐ ☐

Good communication.

☐ ☐

Efficient paperwork.

☐ ☐

Flexibility.

☐ ☐

Broad measurement of the purchasing function (financial and operational)

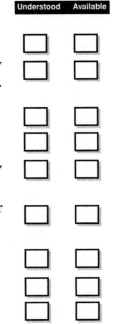

	Understood	Available
Achievement of purchasing budget objectives.	☐	☐
The total costs benefits of the purchasing and supply function, compared with the total costs of purchases.	☐	☐
Reductions in levels of scrap and rework.	☐	☐
Average costs of processing an order.	☐	☐
Cost reductions through supplier development, resourcing or material developments.	☐	☐
Disaggregated cost reviews/improvements for direct and indirect purchasing.	☐	☐
Reductions in number of shortages.	☐	☐
Reductions in supply lead times.	☐	☐
Reduction in supply base	☐	☐

Purchasing strategy

Highlight in the space provided the key objectives of
your company's purchasing strategy:

Is this purchasing strategy communicated to your
suppliers?   ☐   ☐

What results have been achieved from any purchasing strategy implementations over the past:

Six months?   ☐   ☐

One year?   ☐   ☐

Two years?   ☐   ☐

Chapter 27

Checklist: Chapter 12

Supplier partnering principles

	Understood	Available
View the supply base as an integral part of the supply chain game plan strategy.	☐	☐
Establish a customer–supplier partnership business understanding that encompasses a long-term commitment, mutual trust, respect and continuous improvement.	☐	☐
Develop joint continuous development teams looking at improvements within each other's organization.	☐	☐
Develop routines and disciplines for measuring the relationship and the approaches to yielding continuous improvements.	☐	☐
Understand that the supply base as an integral part of the supply chain can only be sustained by profit. The longevity of the relationship is better guaranteed by eliminating waste and improving services.	☐	☐

Defining expectations

	Understood	Available
Clarify communication channels.	☐	☐
Specify order rules.	☐	☐
Clarify total inventory objectives.	☐	☐
Specify logistics flows.	☐	☐
Defined and managed engineering change processes.	☐	☐
Packaging arrangements.	☐	☐
Quality expectations.	☐	☐
Continuous improvement framework.	☐	☐

Supplier development

Supplier development is an ongoing formalized plan for specific improvements and reviews, and might include:

Quality: assured by design and supply.

Delivery: logistics flows, performance improvements, scheduling and materials agreement, minimum lead times/lot sizes/total inventory holding at customer/supplier.

Cost: relationship assessment and strategic review of all business interactions for cost/waste reduction opportunities, including time.

Administration: demand and engineering change management and co-operation and responsiveness. Speed of communication transaction optimization, including EDI, e-mail, web teleconferencing, linked systems.

Technology: business relationship to include proactive technical leadership and product development/feasibility at earliest design stages. Supply partners are actively encouraged to invest in becoming market leaders and continuously innovative.

Attitudes: confident trusting relationship. Information sharing is considerate, timely and accurate. Ethics are considered a major importance for relationship development.

Customer–supplier two-way development assessment (TAIL, 1995)

	Understood	Available
What are the keys to your success?	☐	☐
Why do customers select your products?	☐	☐
What changes do you see in your business?		
What do you see in the future that will change your business?	☐	☐
What are you doing now to prepare for the future?	☐	☐
What are the greatest opportunities for improvement?	☐	☐
What is the one thing that you would like to change?	☐	☐
What can we do to help?	☐	☐
What can we do to make our relationship easier?	☐	☐
What can we do together to reduce costs?	☐	☐
What are the cost drivers?	☐	☐
What can we do together to increase revenues?	☐	☐
What can we do together to increase margins?	☐	☐
What can we do for each other to increase profits?	☐	☐
What can we do for each other to increase growth?	☐	☐

Chapter 28

Checklist: Chapter 13

Logistics management

	Understood	Available
Who manages the logistics function to ensure efficiency and profit?	☐	☐
Does this person have cross-functional authority with responsibility for co-ordinating all logistics?	☐	☐
Are you, or are you in the process of, merging logistics related activities, including:	☐	☐
Marketing.	☐	☐
Production planning.	☐	☐
Transport.	☐	☐
Purchasing/supply.	☐	☐
Storage.	☐	☐
If the answer is 'yes' to the point above, have you set joint targets and objectives between existing functional groups?	☐	☐
Do you have cross-functional project teams tackling individual improvement programmes?	☐	☐

Information handling: addressing order processing policies/ routines

Understood   Available

Does the design of processing routines tie in with the
needs and facilities offered by:

Sales forecasting?

Production planning?

Procurement timescales?

Financial security?

Capacity/nature of distribution?

Benchmark criteria for information flows

	Understood	Available
Who originates and 'owns' the information?	☐	☐
Who needs to receives it?	☐	☐
What is it used for?	☐	☐
When must it be originated and received?	☐	☐
How much time does it take?	☐	☐
What information must be transmitted?	☐	☐
How reliable is the information and the process?	☐	☐
What are the costs?	☐	☐

Examination of information flows

Understood   Available

This allows you to:

Identify important information needs.
☐ ☐

Discard flows that do not add value.
☐ ☐

Speed and automate routine information transactions.
☐ ☐

Address management information systems requirements and decision support systems.
☐ ☐

Transport overview

	Understood	Available
Review current operations/processes.	☐	☐
Design/redesign.	☐	☐
Co-ordinate.	☐	☐
Validate most appropriate modes and service levels.	☐	☐
Automate and audit payment systems for carrier invoices.	☐	☐
Automate invoice data to create standardization and reporting.	☐	☐

Completion of inbound/outbound transport matrix (disaggregating transport movements)

	Understood	Available
Inbound or outbound shipments.	☐	☐
Origin address.	☐	☐
Destination address.	☐	☐
Shipment frequency.	☐	☐
Carrier names.	☐	☐
Delivery service level.	☐	☐
Weights.	☐	☐
Current freight cost.	☐	☐
Model best practice scenarios for returns of parts/bins to suppliers.	☐	☐

Warehousing

	Understood	Available
Does the warehouse location optimize logistics flow (centralized / localized)?	☐	☐
Is the warehouse being used cost-effectively?	☐	☐
Does it allow for adequate access to stored materials?	☐	☐
Is it secure from the weather?	☐	☐
Is it secure from theft?	☐	☐
Is it secure for authoritative management of parts?	☐	☐
Is there enough flexibility for storing the largest and smallest items required?	☐	☐
Third party stocking by part is known, updated and communicated regularly to relevant parties?	☐	☐

Warehouse information systems

	Understood	Available
Stock is put into known places in known order.	☐	☐
Stock is retrieved quickly and in the right quantity.	☐	☐
Stock is rotated properly.	☐	☐
Information systems provide access to occurrences of stock-outs/discrepancies (for root cause analysis).	☐	☐

Materials handling: technological assessment

	Understood	Available
Assessment of the physical characteristics of loads.	☐	☐
The number of loads to be moved.	☐	☐
The distance loads are to be moved.	☐	☐
The speed of movement required.	☐	☐

Materials handling: associated costs

	Understood	Available
What is the cost of building/dismantling loads?	☐	☐
How often does it have to be done?	☐	☐
Does the system impose special packaging requirements?	☐	☐
If yes, what effects does this have on suppliers, transport links, safe storage, stacking, counting and production processes?	☐	☐
How does the system interface with other storage, transport and handling systems used by suppliers and customers?	☐	☐
What are the housekeeping costs of counting, cleaning, heating, cooling, moving goods?	☐	☐

Inventory analysis

	Understood	Available

Do you have available report summaries for ABC classifications or most critical parts/families of inventory?   ☐   ☐

Summarize by stock-keeping units, as a percentage of overall inventory, your current inventory compilation mix for analysis of best practice inventory management:

	Understood	Available
JIT.	☐	☐
Kanban.	☐	☐
MRP.	☐	☐
In transit.	☐	☐
Free-issue.	☐	☐
Work in progress.	☐	☐
Service stock.	☐	☐
Finished stock.	☐	☐
How many stock turns are currently achieved?	☐	☐

Conclusions/remarks:

Current inventory compilation mix 'justification'

Understood   Available

This is explained by:

Cost benefits (bulk buying, etc.). ☐ ☐

Supplier lead times differ from customer lead times. ☐ ☐

An overstated master production schedule. ☐ ☐

Conversion process quality problems. ☐ ☐

'Accepted' safety stock 'just in case'. ☐ ☐

Forecasting uncertainties. ☐ ☐

'Anticipation' stock of free-issue material. ☐ ☐

Supplier geography. ☐ ☐

Supplier quality. ☐ ☐

Supplier minimum order quantities/economic order quantities. ☐ ☐

Poor departmental/external communication. ☐ ☐

Firm period scheduling commitments. ☐ ☐

Conclusions/remarks:

Supply base logistics (balancing the flow between inputs and outputs)

	Understood	Available
Is the geography and/or total lead time taking value/flexibility out of the supply chain?	☐	☐
Identify supply base logistics whose lead times are greater than your supply cycle times.	☐	☐

Evaluation of reasons for this situation are:

	Understood	Available
Price	☐	☐
Specialism of product.	☐	☐
No other supplier available.	☐	☐
Contractual obligations.	☐	☐
Supplier relationship.	☐	☐
Customer product preference.	☐	☐
Intercompany economies of scale.	☐	☐
Consignment stocking.	☐	☐
Political.	☐	☐
Source approval obligation.	☐	☐
Other.	☐	☐

How do your answers compare with the following vendor assessment criteria scenarios:

	Understood	Available
Delivery speed.	☐	☐
Delivery dependability.	☐	☐
Quality.	☐	☐
Route flexibility.	☐	☐
Total cost.	☐	☐

Conclusions/remarks:

Optimizing inventory flow

	Understood	Available
JIT: could most critical parts/families be delivered on a just in time system?	☐	☐
Kanban: where there is a regular demand for a part, could it be delivered on a kanban system?	☐	☐
MRP: address/readdress safety stock formula. Minimum order quantities. Economic order quantities. Manufacturing lead times. Supply total lead time. Firm period schedule commitments. EDI scheduling.	☐	☐
In transit: review invoicing procedures/payment terms. Develop consignment stocking.	☐	☐
Free issue: supplier linking for all free-issue material. If this is not possible formulate a call-off material requirement procedure.	☐	☐
Work in progress (WIP): assign a benchmark value to current WIP (for improvement measurement). Review master production schedule, rough-cut capacity planning. Review work centre capability, routings, set-up times, lot sizes, queues and transit times. Review production scheduling rules, e.g. optimized production technology (OPT), cell manufacturing possibilities.	☐	☐
Service demand: correlate historical data/seasonal variations for forecast planning. If necessary, configure expected demand into safety stock parameters. Set up a service team to communicate/fulfil requirements. Measures for optimization of service level commitments. Collaborate service level policy strategy.	☐	☐
Finished stock: create a generic/modular product. Develop agility into the supply chain strategy.	☐	☐

Just-in-time appraisal

	Understood	Available

Quality: no safety stocks. Deliveries direct to the line. Any quality issues must be eliminated – a prerequisite. ☐ ☐

Speed: very little work in process. This is a work to order system. Some capacity will have to be sacrificed. ☐ ☐

Dependability: dependability of supply, quality, logistics, communication, are prerequisites for fast throughput. ☐ ☐

Flexibility: resultant small batch sizes requires flexibility and consistency throughout the supply chain or decoupling points. ☐ ☐

Optimal inventory flow objectives

	Understood	Available
Increased stock turns.	☐	☐
Balanced customer–supplier lead times.	☐	☐
Order-driven flow versus forecast-driven activity.	☐	☐

Conditions for just-in-time implementation

	Understood	Available
Level schedules.	☐	☐
Reduce set-up times.	☐	☐
Reduce non-value added activities.	☐	☐
Improved process layout and flow.	☐	☐
Design for manufacture.	☐	☐
Total productive maintenance.	☐	☐
Trained people.	☐	☐
Reliable suppliers.	☐	☐

Just-in-time feasibility

Understood   Available

Feasibility example (assumes formalized/computer management system is in place):

Draw up a workflow chart from supplier – transport – receipt.   ☐ ☐

Dismantle the workflow process chart into process segments.   ☐ ☐

Propose new workflow process.   ☐ ☐

Just-in-time feasibility: cost analysis

	Understood	Available
Annualized production (days/weeks/months).	☐	☐
Product build assumptions (days/weeks/months).	☐	☐
Lot-size on-costs.	☐	☐
Average pack weight/density (for transport calculation).	☐	☐
Air-freight/road haulage cost per run.	☐	☐
Packaging/container requirements/costs.	☐	☐
Any additional haulage costs.	☐	☐
Calculate total cost scenario.	☐	☐

Proposed cost benefits against existing workflow process

	Understood	Available

Cost of inventory holding (%).

Labour savings: planning, progressing.

Cost avoidance: panic costs, e.g. air-freight, special deliveries.

Calculate total cost scenario.

Deduct JIT cost analysis scenario.

Total.

If cost analysis is favourable conduct failure mode and effects analysis on proposed workflow.

Consider in conjunction with total JIT benefits.

Implement.

Chapter 29

Checklist: Chapter 14

Distribution resource planning

	Understood	Available
Sales forecasts for stock-keeping units and by distribution centres.	☐	☐
Customer order information for both current and future delivery requirements.	☐	☐
On-hand inventory availability by distribution centre.	☐	☐
Factored availability of outstanding purchase orders or manufacturing orders by product.	☐	☐
Safety stock policies.	☐	☐
Minimum batch quantities.	☐	☐
Logistics, manufacturing and purchase lead times.	☐	☐
Best practice mode of transport and delivery frequency.	☐	☐

Bibliography

Christopher, M. G. (1994). *The Customer Service Planner*. Butterworth-Heinemann.

Christopher, M. G. (1991). *Relationship Marketing*. Butterworth-Heinemann.

Croner (1999). *Manufacturing Operations, Management and Practice*.

Economic Intelligence Unit (EIU) (1995). *Supply Chain Management*. EIU.

Ford, H. (1998). *Today and Tomorrow*. Reprint edition. Productivity Press.

Forrester, J. (1961). *Industrial Dynamics*. MIT Press.

Jina, J. (1996). Getting value time in the supply chain. *Control*, May.

Kruse, G. et al. (1996) Predicting the future: Forecasting issues, problems and ideas. *Control*, November.

Mather, H. (1998). How to profitably delight your customers. *Control*, October, 16–20.

Newberry. T. L. and Bhame, C. D. (1981). How management should use and interact with sales forecasts. *Inventories and Production Magazine*, July–August.

Peters, M. J. and Wright, D. S. (1999). *A Research Report on International Air Express Distribution*. Cranfield University.

Pine, B. J. II (1993). *Mass Customization, the New Frontier in Business Competition*. Harvard Business School Press.

Producer Responsibility Obligations (packaging waste) (1997). UK leglisation

Robertson, M., Swan, J. and Newel, S. (1997). The spread of technologies to support operations management. *Control*, March.

Sako, M. (1992). *Buyer, Suppliers, and Trust in Japanese Business*. Sterling.

Smith, P. G. and Reinertsen, D. G. (1991). *Developing Products in Half the Time*. van Nostrand Reinhold.

Society of British Aerospace Companies (SBAC) (1996). Report on the Procurement Process within the Aerospace Industry. SBAC.

Suzaski, K. (1993). *The New Shop Floor Management*. Free Press.

Tompkins Associates International Ltd (TAIL) (1995). *Partnership: A Commitment to Excellence*. TAIL.

Tompkins, J. A. (1989). *Winning Manufacturing: The How-To Book of Successful Manufacturing*. Industrial Engineering and Management Press.

University of Westminster, supported by Institute of Logistics and Transport (1998). The UK packaging waste regulations: the implications for freight transport and logistics, *Logistics Focus*, June.

Womack, J. P., Jones, D. T. and Roos, D. (1990). *The Machine that Changed the World*. Macmillan.

Index

Printed in the United Kingdom
by Lightning Source UK Ltd.
111287UKS00001BA/9